READ BETWEEN THE LINES OF MANAGEMENT

UNDERSTANDING THE NUANCES

RAJENDRA CHANDORKAR

Copyright © Rajendra Chandorkar
All Rights Reserved.

This book has been published with all efforts taken to make the material error-free after the consent of the author. However, the author and the publisher do not assume and hereby disclaim any liability to any party for any loss, damage, or disruption caused by errors or omissions, whether such errors or omissions result from negligence, accident, or any other cause.

While every effort has been made to avoid any mistake or omission, this publication is being sold on the condition and understanding that neither the author nor the publishers or printers would be liable in any manner to any person by reason of any mistake or omission in this publication or for any action taken or omitted to be taken or advice rendered or accepted on the basis of this work. For any defect in printing or binding the publishers will be liable only to replace the defective copy by another copy of this work then available.

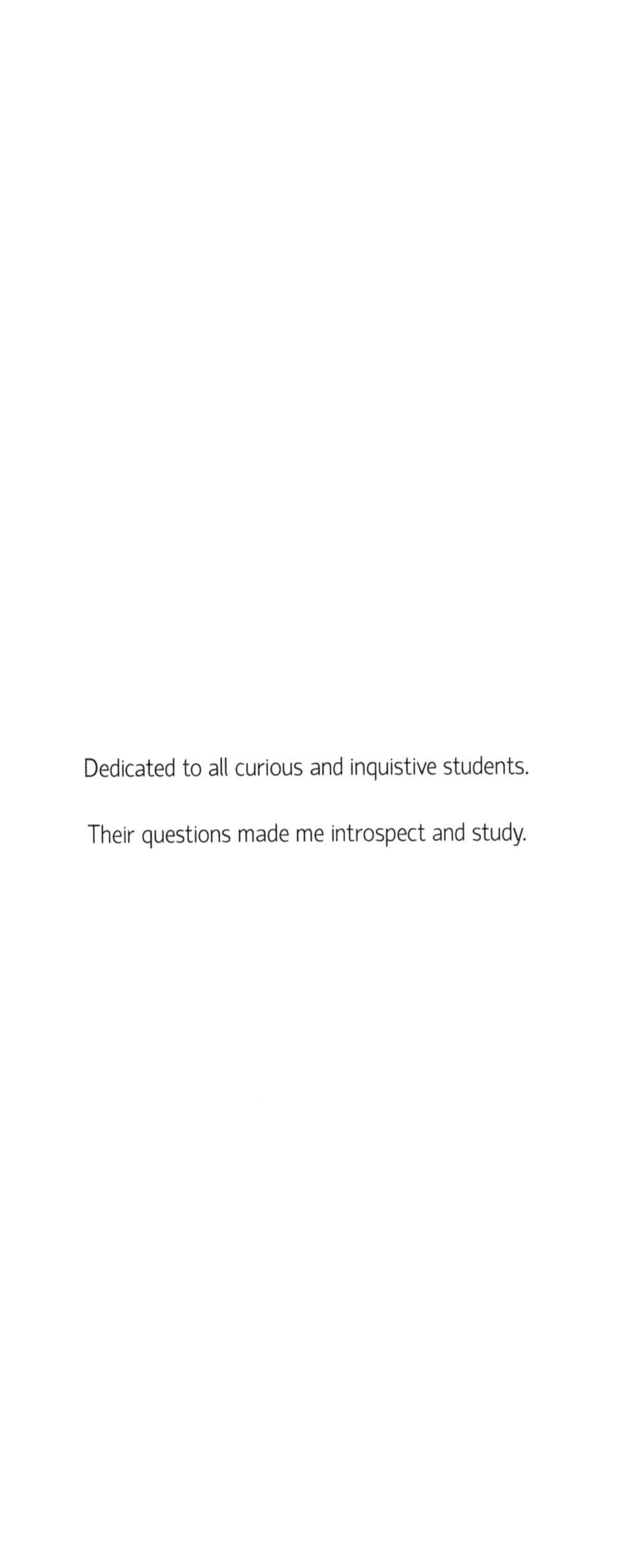

Dedicated to all curious and inquistive students.

Their questions made me introspect and study.

Contents

Contents

Foreword

My education about formal management started in 1977. Thanks to my teachers I could pick up some invaluable basics. The study continues and I am very thankful to all those who thought that I am a person who can answer their queries.

What Fayol or Drucker promoted is very significant and we must be grateful for thier immense and almosr irreplaceable contribution in the field of formal management. We must understnd that the world, before the formal onset of management, definitely had their own systems which were pretty successful. in the absence of communication media they could effectively trade and travel across the world they knew. In India, every mamangement graduate faces an acid test when he starts to interact with the actual market, clients and customers. The contrast he faces is simply incredible. At times, he starts doubting what he had learnt in the management courses.

Application of any thing, whether theory or practicals, we learn in our colleges checks out our comprehension of the said topic. It cuts in two ways, one way tells us how we can do it and the other tells how it cannot be done. Indian managers spend their maximum time in listening to how the things cannot be done. Further coupled with ridicule and a blunt oblique refernce to the formal management. Only one way he can respond is by trying out his conviction and prove his detractors wrong. In fact, one of my teachers asked us to get the photographs of all such people and hang them on our walls. He further told us that there can be no more inspiration than such faces. I tried, in the later years and believe me it works. Doing <u>improbable assignments</u> paves the way for achieving the proverbial IMPOSSIBLE.

If we compare management with the medical profession where they study the standard structure of human body, its variations and possible complications. Some seven billions humans live on the planet earth have common features and yet each is different sample.

The common basis which they learnt in the medical schools has to be customised for each of the patient and the diagnosis is arrived at. Compared to them the managers have a slightly easier job to do. at least they are not dealing with a beating heart and pusating lungs. But that does not mean that they can relax. The scales of the decisions these days where we are talking of billions can be a great stress.

Again the only ally of the practicing manager is his implicit belief in what he had learnt and its crediblity. One factor keeps him performing..." if he cannot somebody else will and he would be left far behind". Each problem, (oh no, now they refer the problems as challenges, they tell me that the problems sound more harsh than challenges. Challenges can be overcome.) presents an opportunity to the operating manager to try some concept in the management education. Each success would prove to be milestone in his long and ardupous career. As he comes of age he starts acquring more taste and flavours. He starts to become more complete and more ready for the next challenge.

A true and hard core manager never retires, he keeps on and on.

***

Acknowledgements

I acknowledge with a lot of pride the help offered by my colleageus and seniors. I can name at least a hundred form whom I learnt the tricks of the trade, but there would be many more who would be missed, so I just thank each and every one who helped me to grow, achieve some success.

My students helped me grow as they had very little faith in anything good. They did not say so but their eyes told me that they face more hazardous times than me and my generation. Last seventy years of Independence in India has created a success model in which corruption amd malpractices rule supreme. I thank all those who prevented me from falling in the trap.

I cannot close this page without acknowledging the correct teachings given to me by my teachers. They were so big hearted that their graces would make the oceans appear small. They had solutions to each doubt raised by me and my fellow students and they openly shared their wisdom. The difference between the knowledge and the proverbial wisdom was made crystal clear by them.

I thank all my friends who have more confidence in my capability than me and they keep telling me to share my experiences.

Rajendra Chandorkar.

CHAPTER ONE

ABOUT DREAMS

<u>About Dreams</u>

There is a famous pop song, "I have a dream" by the famous Rock group Abba. It created great waves. People started talking about dreams, their relevance and their necessity in the human life and performance of persons. The theory of an American dream was also in vogue. Dreams were promoted; persons with dreams were called as visionaries.

Shift the scene to a common man. The question "What is your dream?" makes him, more often than not, very conscious and acutely uncomfortable. What has dream got to do with a normal life, is what he tends to think. He prides himself to be a *rational* and a practical person who deals in reality of the life. Being as near as phlegmatic is his usual guard against the over curious and pushy people. So, when put to talk about dreams he is not at all ready. Why should he discuss with anyone the most secret part of his life with anyone? It is also matter of trust or more likely lack of trust. There is impending fear of ridicule and almost a guarantee of a "Look who is talking".

Dream is a word which makes you self-conscious. Is it because of the fact that it may remind you of all the things which you wanted to achieve but could not? Does it remind you of all the petty adjustments for leading a supposedly normal life? You start thinking and you would know that you cannot isolate yourself from the word dream. You are either working for accomplishment of your dream (if you belong to a cadre of a select few) or you are working for someone to achieve his dream. So, in short you have your dream or you are a part of some one's dream. The choice is always yours.

Dream is something we automatically associate with sleep and because of this we rarely give any importance to what we see in our dreams. But dreams deserve a better deal. Whatever we have done is our past, whatever we do today is our present, but the only way we can live in future is in our dreams. It is a great thing. And to make the dreams better we can shape, paint and crystallize them in any way we want. It is accepted that what we see in our dreams is what we think. The possibility factor rarely matters in the dreams.

What are dreams?

People have various impressions. For some dream is the basis of the future. For some it is a fickle mind's expression. Some feel that the dreams are invaluable others term them as a worthless activity. The dreaming can be like a dream while some one is sleeping, day dreaming, nightmares, and sweet dreams like in a romantic novel, dream as an objective, and dream as a vision. The dream is something most people like to talk about when they are proclaimed as successful and that is right too. Everyone is interested in some body and his dreams if and only if he succeeds.

A person who dreams and then does nothing about it is *not the person* we wish to discuss here. We are looking into the persona of those who dream and subsequently realize the same. Very rarely, people have fixed dreams. It is seen that the dreams evolve with the time and circumstances.

There is a story which explains the aspect in the discussion. Once, there was a big fight between the Dream and the Truth. The issue was as usual about being more powerful. Both fought bitterly but could not reach a decision. So, they approached the God. He listened to what they had to say. He smiled and said "I am throwing my wand in the space, and let me see who catches it? Up went the wand in the space. The Truth tried, very hard, stretching it self to the fullest but could not even touch. It was crest fallen and disappointed. The Dream just zoomed and caught the wand. It was very excited. It expected some praise from Him. The God said "You both have failed. The truth could not even touch the wand. The dream *reached the wand* but its feet were off the ground."

The dreams of a common man and the men who are termed as more than equals have different futures. The common man dreams and then starts finding reasons for the expected failures. More often than not he does not realize that if he can dream something he himself is responsible for the success of the dream. Not in the cases of powerful people. John F Kennedy, the President of America, in one of the public addresses given in 1962 said that US would put a man on the moon before the end of the decade. The press, as well as the wise people from NASA were all equally nonplussed. They asked the President if he had any information, any plan for the same. The President disarmingly said that he just knew. The statement set the ball in the motion and the first human, Neil Armstrong walked on the moon, in July 1969.

So, the dream which matters is what you see as your future with your feet firmly grounded. The dreaming is not to be confused with wishful thinking, which most of us do. When the dream is more aligned towards the aim it becomes more relevant. There is only one difference between the dream and the aim. *The dream requires effortless sleep whereas the aim requires sleepless efforts.* They say that *sleep* for a dream and *wake up* for an aim.

Once you dream, it is your baby. You have to nurture, care and fight for the same. If you do not accomplish what you dream you alone are responsible. Get away from those who tell you that you cannot do it. Get away from the dream killers who are dime a dozen in all parts of the world.

So finally, we have to understand that the dream is the beginning of any endeavor. To begin with the dream may not have any limits, no thoughts of finance or for that matter any other known resource, but in itself the dream does not have capacity to achieve anything. It requires logic, efforts, feasibility as its complements to survive and succeed. A mere dream can never match the glory of an accomplished dream.

The dream is inherently a positive term. It includes means to help the mankind. It is designed in such a way that mankind benefits from the dream. There are many in the history who are discredited despite of their huge successes solely because their dreams were hazardous the overall good of the human interests. The poetic dreaminess is usually a failure unless it is concretely supported by the steely resolve of an active workman like approach. One small step towards the final achievement is enough to finally reach the destination.

So, dream, dream big and achieve big.

***

CHAPTER TWO

Benchmarks

Some terms enjoy a special preference in modern management lingo. Benchmark is one of them.

We in our professional lives have talked about the benchmarks mostly at the times of annual reviews. The accepted benchmark in most cases is dependent upon the performance or to be more correct the peak performance of the last year. Whatever was the best automatically is the benchmark this year. You start from the best last year and try to better it for setting up the new benchmark. The whole system is aligned as per the recently set bench marks and the ball is rolled for the play.

Classically benchmarks are very ordinary and have been mainly used to demarcate heights of the structures. A bench mark usually means a horizontal line with an arrow pointing up from below. These marks were cut by Ordnance Survey leveling staff to provide a network of points at which the height has been precisely measured (to the centre of the horizontal line) above sea level. It is estimated that millions of such bench marks exist, but now they have outlived their importance and almost half have disappeared. You may still find them mainly on buildings (especially churches) and on bridges. The importance of benchmarks originates from their constant nature. Whoever and however he counts the value of the concerned benchmark always remains constant. But then these are with respect to the 'non living' standards. As soon as the living are included and that too humans, the nature of the term undergoes a change. Or if the term does not assume different meaning, then the measurement systems definitely do.

The benchmarks in absolute scale are very rarely seen these days and that is why probably the term is used as a means of moderation rather than as a pure performance check. The dilution in selective cases where in the benchmarks are lowered creates an inferior end result. In any organization whether an office or a nation we are sure to find people for whom there are differential bench marks and further these people are creating a lot of hurdles in a smooth functioning of the system. This begins right at the elementary level and persists till the "illogical" and expected end of the process. No one has time and daring to address the core problem of diluted benchmarks and more often than not the people with proper skills double for these diluted versions.

The cardinal sin of lowering the benchmark that too as an ad hoc choice has been done more as a popular measure than as a proper one, we are not ready to spare the premier institutions like IITs, IIMs, and Medical Colleges and are bent upon converting them into the ordinary ones. The logic of the people for asking the lowering of benchmark is as funny as the people themselves. They say that people find it difficult to get admissions in these colleges, but then that was the **original idea.** Wasn't it? The rarity of the gem stone makes it expensive and exclusive. If diamonds are found every where what would be their value?

To extend the logic a little further I would like to cite the example of the pearls. A pearl is formed when some sort of small object, gets embedded in the tissue of an oyster. In response, probably as a defense mechanism the mantle tissue of the mollusk secretes nacre, which is mix of calcium carbonate and a fibrous protein called conchiolin. This was accepted as a rare occurrence and the pearl thus formed yielded high value. It was slightly irregular and of various shades of white. People wanted more pearls and hence started culturing pearls. The concept of cultured pearls is deliberately inserting a foreign object into the tissue of an oyster; culturists can induce the creation of a pearl. The same natural process of pearl creation takes place. Today it is estimated that more than 95% of the pearls are cultured. You have pearls but are they equally valuable as the natural ones?

One more example from a totally different field, but is acknowledged as one which requires maximum management principles. In Cricket, what Sir Don Bradman achieved is a serious benchmark, an average of 99.6, with 29 Centuries, in a meager 52 tests. He played when there were no helmets, the pitches were not covered, and traveling was tedious and hazardous. Subsequently, there were many who were talked about as the 'near' and 'new' Bradman. But when compared with the benchmark of 99.96 each one faded fast.

In future, India would have huge number of very 'qualified' people but the outputs are expected to be at minimum, as the qualifications would be a result of *diluted benchmarks*. Already we are facing this problem and in future we should be ready to face even worse situations. The original benchmarks would be lost, discarded as the tough ones, the newer one would not be relevant and the expectations would ask for a moon. Lowering benchmarks can be compared to call any hillock in your town as the Mount Everest and climb it. You know what you have done and the world would certainly laugh at you. Do not feel bad, you have lot of company. It is promoted that because you can not do something, you feel that it is out of bounds for you, so dilute the same and talk about the new 'achievements.

Benchmarking in management has evolved as a definite tool for appraisals and decision making. It has resulted in re-invention, re-engineering, downsizing, cutback management, and a close public scrutiny. Benchmarking can be defined as an ongoing systematic process for **measuring and comparing** the work processes of one organization to those of another for the purpose of identifying best practices that can lead to improvements in operations and customer service. The benchmarking serves as intra-organization tool and this is where real an objective management is expected but rarely met.

Success would never lower its standards to accommodate us. We have to raise ourselves to achieve. They say that God provides the food to every 'beak' but please note, not in the nest of the bird.

So, move out, struggle, and create benchmarks of your own which would be the starting points for many others, for many centuries to come.

***

10000 runs! A real Benchmark by Great Sunil Gavaskar

CHAPTER THREE

Beyond Fifteen Minutes Smartness.

Due to the information technology explosion in the recent past quite a few things have come out in the open. The first to stand out is that every person has become smarter than his *earlier* version. You may have realized the same! Do you agree? Good! The earlier version was a labored, nervous and may be slightly unsure about his thoughts and position, not so now. The information provided by the TV channels, by way of the news, interviews, panel discussions, features, live telecasts, as well as by the print media acts as a revitalizer at least on a marginal level. It is so easy! Whether you want to know about your falling incomes or falling hair or even your falling standards of morals and ethics, be sure that you have a readymade, easy to consume, shortcut dose of advice. Take any area in your life and you have it repaired or re-oriented by some smart Alec who tells you "How to". The easy access has arguably devalued the importance of the information.

I am in the exposure of such people and I feel that it is as bad as the Uranium radiation. I am amused to see the changes in people around me. To a certain extent I am happy for such changes in people and their improved behavior. What makes me sad is that these changes are predominantly on the exterior side, and more often than not on a cosmetic scale. They are now better dressed, better in their usual conversations or in the routine interactions with other people. However, it becomes a time consuming, if not time-wasting exercise, as you venture to find out *the real value* of these people. This is the reason, why most times you feel mildly cheated, when you find a person whom you thought to be a smart one, fades out very fast. The problem becomes even more serious when the person in question is your employee or a colleague and further worse *if your performance depends* on him. We come across such problematic people in our active careers. They are in abundance in lower, middle and higher levels of management. The decision making becomes the first casualty at the hands of such people. When I discussed this problem with my friends and associates, I was surprised to receive very animated response. They readily accepted the presence and discussed their torture at the hands of these people.

Such persons are categorized in a slightly new concept named as Fifteen Minutes Smart, the FMS.

The surface levels at which these FMS are accustomed to operate can be deceptive and it takes an astute and experienced person to appraise such FMS. The FMS, unfortunately, are in a majority these days. Hence, what I *write is for the ones who believe* in the hard earned, slogged for and time-consuming version of the smartness. They are the ones who are left with proverbial cleaning operations.

Let us find out the characteristics of the FMS. The first is that FMS are overdressed. They are loud in their bearing. They speak very loudly, and try to dominate the meetings. They have an acceptable command over the language they speak. They can speak on any topic for a short time, restricting the talk to the generalities. They speak in the words of someone else and never acknowledge. They would rarely accept what others have to say, but when it comes to deliver, they would invariably do the vanishing trick.

They can be extremely sly and are prone to taking the shortcuts. They are willing to help only those persons who are good looking, fair and usually belong to the fairer sex. They shall do this holy thing at a serious cost of their colleagues. They speak poison for their *friends,* and not at all bothered by the inner voice. Their receiver may not have this channel.

They are very poor timekeepers, and come late to the meetings and subsequently give some unimaginable reason. But if the Big Man calls the meeting, then they arrive on time and can look very busy. Overall, they give a restless appearance. They can move at a break neck speed here and there, without actually doing anything worthwhile. They are shallow and this shows to all those who have some time and inclination to test out these people. The thing that works in the cases of FMS, is that the ones who matter, do not generally have time to test the FMS. Actually, after a few interactions with the FMS I have seriously stopped believing in the *first impressions*. The FMS are masters in pleasing the bosses. They make it a point to know everything about the boss, as well as the boss of the boss, the wife of the boss. They keep a track of the birthdays, and other important days in the life of the boss. Do not confuse FMS with the *chamchas*, as the FMS are smarter and sure of what they want and to get them in any which way possible, ignoring the accepted norms.

FMS are masters in positive "talking". As long as they have to only talk, they would promise every one every thing. The distance between the talking and the actual doing is very rarely traveled by the FMS. They boom in the meetings and can monopolize them. Under the garb of the positive thinking, they talk of goals. The more impossible nature of the goal suits better to these people. After all they are not going to put any effort to achieve the goals. They know that when such time arrives, they would not be around.

FMS can be extremely irritating to the prudent ones. The prudent think before they talk and hence find FMS as loveable as the plague. Because they cannot assert and resist, they have to temporarily accept all the trash dished out by the FMS.

FMS are blessed with a very selective memory. They remember the shortcomings of their colleagues. They have an uncanny knack of presenting the awkward data at the most inopportune time for sincere workers. (Since the time of the early civilizations, it is proved that those who are sincere workers or have a different vision have to swim against the current.) The selective memory very conveniently allows the FMS to forget his promises and failures.

What happens to the FMS in the end? Do people like them or just tolerate them? How do they function in a team? Until what time such shortcuts can be effective? What about the core? You have to decide for your specific cases.

There is no substitute for the old-fashioned and simple hard work. "Do it yourself" is the first condition, which starts the downfall of the FMS. When it comes to actually doing something the FMS is at a loss, for the simple reason that he does not know how to do anything or even worse there is a lack of inclination. Therefore, once again he tries his time-tested method of finding a person who may actually do the job. As soon as the job is done with FMS moves in like a hyena and grabs the credit. Sadly, for the FMS, his organization cannot have an unending supply of doers who are gullible. There comes a time when every one in the organization becomes wise and then the only way for the FMS is the way out.

Actually, FMS should understand one simple thing. Doing something is most of the times easier than the manipulations the FMS undertakes. Rarely, the FMS accept this. Moreover, the satisfaction of an accomplishment and the purest joy of doing cannot be replaced. Couple this with all the ill feelings generated in the minds of the FMS victims, and the picture becomes clearer. For his own self-esteem the FMS should find out the benefit of an honest effort as against the manipulation of the people.

We have to seriously reorient our methods of the selection and the subsequent appraisals to weed out the FMS. The new system should be designed in such a way that it enables us to filter such garbage before it can further vitiate our organizations and the society. We already know that there is very little connection between the qualifications the person has and his actual capacity to deliver the goods. This is reflected in the individual and customized entrance as well as aptitude tests conducted by various industries, which are reluctant to take the qualifications on their face value.

***

CHAPTER FOUR

Beyond the Positive Thinking.

It is generally accepted that the great thinker Norman Vincent Peale first enunciated the concept of positive thinking in the late forties of the last century. It was received with a great enthusiasm and fanfare. Many said that the problems of human motivation would be almost taken care of, if we all use the concept in a right way. It was acclaimed as a master key to all problems. Sixty years down the line, a fresh view is needed. While accepting the basic concept, we have to find whether it really helps a person to find success after he thinks positively. The path to success has various milestones and each of them is significant. Positive thinking is one of the major factors and hence should be studied in details. Last few decades have produced so many motivational experts (with absolute and questionable expertise) who have been very candid about the concept of positive thinking. They have written books, delivered seminars and generally have made every sensible person aware about immense value of positive thinking.

The simplest definition of positive and negative can be: Positive is what you like, while Negative is what you do not like. It may not be always pertinent but can act as a starter for subsequent discussion. There are things which you do not like, yet you know that they are right. What do you think about them?

Are you a positive thinker? Just check it out!

Are you confident and self-assured?

Is your thinking constructive and productive?

When evaluating a situation, do you focus on the brighter side?

Do you think in terms accomplishing the task?

Do you focus on how things *can* be done—and *make* them happen.

We all know that when we feel positive, we feel relaxed and perform better whatever we're doing. Trouble is that always looking for the brighter side of life is easier said than done. However, you would feel better if you know that you do not need any particular skills or to go on any special course for being a positive thinker. Once you accept, you can transform your present un preconditioned self in to a more acceptable positive version. It is more of conditioning rather than learning some thing new.

In today's ruthless corporate world, a positive attitude is increasingly one of the most important and foremost weapons for survival. At work places, such qualities as 'the ability to motivate', 'excellent communication skills', 'able to initiate and manage change' are much in demand. For some, positive thinking comes naturally. The good news for the rest is that, even if it doesn't come naturally, you can learn to be positive.

Does positive thinking mean walking around with a fixed grin all day? A truly positive person recognizes the negatives that crop up day to day, but has the skills and attitude to handle them. He tackles the negatives without any fuss. In fact, he accepts them as a part of the projects.

Positive thinking can be compared to an umbrella. The umbrella cannot stop the rain but it protects us from the rain. Similarly, positive thinking may not always bring us the success, but it gives us the confidence to face all the expected and unexpected challenges.

The process of positive thinking has to be understood.

The first part of positive thinking is to think positively. It must be understood that to think in any way you may like usually should take same efforts. Whether you accept or condemn any concept, event, process, person you still would have spent same amount of time. When you see the proverbial glass filled with water what you see? Do you see "Half full or half empty?". In the recent years people have seen many different ways and have even finished the half glass of water.

The second part of the process is to talk positively. The rule here is if you can not talk good, shut up. If you think the glass is half empty, keep mum for the sake of those who think that it is half full. The fact that the negatives have a tendency to multiply, that too geometrically, should be at the top of your mind.

The third part is the most important and often forgotten is to act positively. What you do to fill the glass is any times more important than just a comment about its emptiness. Do you have any time-tested method to retrieve the situation or you are going in the post mortem mode of why the glass has been empty? The most important thing about positive doing is whether you start the retrieval action or wait for some one else to act. They say that 'lucky' is the one who gets opportunities, 'great' is the one creates opportunities and the 'winner' is the one who uses the opportunity in way it should be. So, from 'getting' to 'winning' the most important step is to act.

The above three things are extremely important in the order given. It is found that any one, if missing, can create a failure. You can think, talk positively but if you do not act in a required manner, you ever could turn in to a winning outfit. The major worry noted in the recent years that most of the people have some how achieved the surface level awareness in the process of positive thinking and they create more problems than the acknowledged cynically negative persons.

One very interesting aspect of the positive thinking is the corporate variety. The rules here are very different. The positive thinking concept has to adjust with another very strong concept which is "The boss is always right". The emerging conflict is very intense and can be a major factor resulting in the success or failure. There is a tremendous confusion about how to respond when the boss is telling some thing which one does not agree. If you disagree you are straight way branded as the negative and if you agree you feel that you are cheating the organization. Very few bosses are ready for listening to a reasonable dissent. They do ask of the employees for their views on any project or process, but inwardly expect every subordinate to agree with what they have to say. This may be the single largest factor for the unsatisfying scene at the corporate levels. The rule here is to follow whatever your conscience tells you. By agreeing to some thing wrong, you are just delaying the inevitable for a temporary respite.

So, be clear in mind that there is a world beyond positive thinking, which promotes action. No one achieves any thing spectacular just by desire. It is a mere starting point, suitable plan and sustained effort must follow the desire. To understand that as any other concept the positive thinking also has its inherent limitations is very important. To succeed we must remember that it is not enough just to aim at some thing, but we have to hit it, that too a Bull's Eye.

***

CHAPTER FIVE

Bottlenecks

Some terms have achieved almost enviable significance over last few years. Innovative, proactive, competencies, benchmarking, broad-banding, change management, emotional intelligence, Hawthorne effect and database, are the words which are used by management professionals day in and day out.

Bottleneck is one more such term which if not used in a management meeting it seems incomplete. The irony is probably that these terms are used more often than not for justifying the failures, rather than as a strategy for success.

Bottleneck is a term which is defined as a phenomenon by which the performance or capacity of an entire system is severely limited by a single component. The component is sometimes called a **bottleneck point**. The term is metaphorically derived from the neck of a bottle, where the flow speed of the liquid is limited by its neck.

To explain the term in its classical sense we can use the simple example of a narrow bridge on an otherwise express highway. Or a single railway track between two stations. The system has every thing else in place but cannot perform at the peak level.

We talk of bottlenecks as if we are the only and probably the first generation of the humans who have encountered bottlenecks and we some how naively expect that because we are intelligent enough to know that we have encountered the bottlenecks, every thing else should be forgiven. All processes have to have certain bottlenecks and the action plan should be flexible enough to accomplish success with the available variety of bottlenecks. The skills as and when available of the managers these days are more utilized in finding out what can not be done and why. The biggest key word in such cases is the 'bottlenecks. The worst development is that the level of people who discuss, argue changes but the reasons/ bottlenecks practically remain same. Solutions for overcoming the bottlenecks are conspicuous by their absence. The effects of such managers and their operations are already visible and most senior managers express their worries, though for obvious reasons they would avoid direct answers, about the quality of the people they have to work with.

Why there should be any bottlenecks in the first place? What is the genesis? If a system is designed, tested, simulated by the experts and then put to use ideally there should be no scope of such things. The planning stage where people are supposed to peep into future and fortify the proposed process against the critical factors is the most likely main breeding ground of the bottlenecks. May be some things are overlooked, may be there is a tremendous pressure of the deadlines, may be the original visionary is no more with the organization and many such 'may be' s can be subsequently identified and submitted at the reviews. But this is at the irrecoverable cost of time and other resources. The original system probably can never be reconstructed and the firefighting exercise for solutions of the arisen bottlenecks takes the centre stage. Naturally the priorities have changed and it usually results in inordinate delays and cost escalations. Mind you the original planning was exactly for the opposite. The planning is for a perfect finish and yet in spite of all planning usually there is bitter end instead of sweet finish.

What can be done? Can we use the bottlenecks and some how control the system in question? For example, the bottleneck places in the course of a river are the best sites for the bridges. Can we act and dilute the effect of the bottlenecks? Can we actually bypass the neck area? Can we develop any strategy where in if the current bottlenecks are taken care of the future can be relatively hassle free?

The answers to these questions and a few more specific to your own situations can decide whether or not the system would work or not in a way it should be.

The severity of the bottlenecks is directly proportional to the number of agencies involved and their participation or more correctly lack of participation. More agencies mean more bottlenecks which are responsible for pending issues and when they cross with the bottlenecks of all others the chaos is to be seen to be believed. For examples all Railway Over Bridges, underground cabling involving three or more government departments, the usual tussle between the finance and operations creates a huge friction and delay the process. The irony in all this is that every one feels that he is doing his duty and best for the company or the country and yet the overall picture is forgotten. When the 'personal scores to be settled' enter the stage, the issues are blown out of proportions and subsequently only post-mortems are possible, which in most cases lead to some more bottlenecks.

People working in traffic managements, computer software designing, railways, power distribution, milk procurements have a longstanding fight with the bottlenecks. They seem to do things right but are always apprehensive about the next day. 'There is no guaranty' they confess that the next day would pass peacefully. The amount of the stress created and not tackled can lead to a very sorry state of affairs.

While facing the classical bottlenecks the team must remember that the problem is almost at end of the road. They have been doing things right in the recent past which has resulted in reaching the bottlenecks. It is a passing phase and if the team persists very soon, they would be laughing about the same bottleneck when celebrating the success of the project.

***

CHAPTER SIX

Communication: A matter of concern

<u>**Really speaking,**</u> are we at cross roads as far as communication is concerned?

So many coaching classes, training sessions, interactive seminars and crash courses claim to improve communication skills of a person, but to what effect is a matter of conjecture. I, as a trainer and teacher have my own share of the woes and in some few cases, of success.

Simply put, communication comprises of a code (message), a medium, dispatcher and a receiver. Each stage has many sub-stages and can be reasons for the success or failure of communication process as a whole. There are white, black and grey areas which need some immediate attention or else we are looking down at a barrel. We are trying for the betterment of communication through some typical observations.

<u>**Confusions and misunderstandings:**</u> There are many confusions regarding communication as a process, carefully created over the years by the populist socialists.

1. <u>The language</u>. The sacredness and sanctity of the language is diluted. I mean any language across the country. Very few in our country can read, write and speak even in their own language at an acceptable level. This aspect of education needs some serious introspection otherwise we would have a permanent damage.

When we refer to English it becomes further discouraging. The total lack of grammar is alarming. Somehow, the lack lustre attitude towards the insistence of the correct language is showing in the day to day working of the offices and government departments. The use of computers has created more confusion. The computer is not worried about 'complement' instead of 'compliment' and you are paying the same to whom. Very few are aware about the feature of spell checks. There is a marked tendency to use 'the cut, copy and paste' as an easy way out. There are thousand mistakes which are tolerated, many more are not even noticed. I remember that one noted English daily used to give Rs. 100 per mistake to any person who reported. If the same arrangement is to be continued, I am sure that millions would be disbursed annually. *'Dicipline'* instead of discipline, *summar* instead of summer, *peak* instead of pick, are a few examples. The scant respect for the language is repaid to the society with a compound interest. **How communication that too effective can be achieved without proper language is a matter beyond comprehension**. Any language has some basic rules, which are patently flaunted and success is expected. We are still tottering at the basic steps trying to improve the elementary standards of language and at the present stage we probably cannot even think of finer nuances required for any intended advancements. <u>That language has to be used in a correct manner is athing of past, at least it is projected so</u>. The smart operators stretch beyond limits to undermine the significance of grammar, comprehension, sentence formation and fill in their coffers at the expense of the poor quality of education which is still somehow available in traces across our country. So let us for once accept that without proper language, decency in communication can not be achieved.

1. <u>Some people</u> claim that they can understand but not speak, read but cannot write and for such a situation they start blaming the system. They always forget that the system was never used by them. They never paid attention to what their teachers desperately tried to teach them. They never have opened

relevant text books; never have taken the exams seriously. They always prepared for the exams to clear with mere passing marks. 40 % was good for them. However, when the scene changes for a possible employment and they demand that they should get what the topper gets (after all India is socialistic country) and try to find out any available shortcuts. Paying huge amount to any one who promised them that what ever they are they would be treated and owing to the shortcut treatments they would get the jobs. The root of all corruption is probably in getting **some paper** which states that one is '**legally**' qualified. Then the scams of fake mark sheets, fake degrees, contacting the evaluators and paying them for more marks, rock the education. That after getting employed one has to work and for that he would need the communication <u>is not at all in the picture</u>. The sole objective of getting a degree is achieved. The paper says so. Such people are always a target for fun and jest. They cannot write a simple application for a casual leave. The basic foundation is missing and they want to construct a building and further expect it to last for ever. What a joke?

2. <u>When the</u> students see that their parents, teachers, bosses and leaders get away without proper communication skills it further damages the situation. 'If he can be a boss without proper communication' the student thinks 'why should I waste time in learning the communication?' Managing without communication is a new trend and it is destroying the basic fabric of decency and decorum. The meetings, the seminars most of the times turn into a farce. The spoiling and degrading language is evident in all walks of life and the future looks hazy.

3. <u>What is popular</u> is not always proper. The students are told by their teachers that the language was created first, in an ad-hoc manner and subsequently the grammar followed. No issues on this statement. May be, it is true! Further the argument that a child does not know grammar and yet it speaks the language. The child apes its parents. This in itself prompts that the parents should speak in a decent way. If they are bad their copies would

be bad too. We have to ask a counter question to such people. Do they want to communicate in a manner their child communicates? Most of the times, what the child speaks is a matter of entertainment for the elders. We fuss over them, we enjoy the effort and we take pride, just like the father in the recent advertisement who is expecting his toddler to say Czechoslovakia. We have to make sure that the communication is not a child's play. To understand the process (which helps a student to speak, write and read properly) is long stretched and requires some serious effort on the parts of the student, teachers and the parents. Sadly, all three stake holders are not doing enough and hence the present situation emerges, where in the people with degrees and post graduate degrees can not communicate in a manner befitting to their degrees.

4. <u>What can be done?</u> In fact, quite a few things, such as to stop playing with examination styles and pattern. The newer patterns are more often than not worse than the previous ones. Secondly, there should be no upwards pushing of the students. There must be as many exams as possible and only those who clear them should be promoted, irrespective of any class or creed. Whether the exams are held in a traditional one-time evaluation or based on the continuous evaluation pattern they should be in right spirit and the process should be really monitored so as to be more effective and productive. The students must understand that if they do not achieve the required standards, they would not be gifted with degrees. Any evaluation should give due credit to intelligence of a person rather than the short comings. 'Honest' teachers are available even today (though they are a vanishing tribe) must be rewarded. The rewards should have some significance, unlike what is prevalent today. In due course of time, we would again have students who are worthy enough of their degrees. Any other compromise would kill the language and subsequently the communication.

5. <u>Whether the receiver is ready?</u> As a major stake holder of the communication processes, the receiver is most of the times a

neglected entity. The politician talking to the *janata*, the teachers talking to students, salesman talking to customer very rarely check for this important aspect. The results are to be seen these days. The intensity levels may not exist. The listeners as well as talkers lack the basic virtue, which is patience. The levels are not maintained and at the first chance the same are lowered further. The populist measures would be the last nail in the communication coffin. There seems to be a mad race for getting the hammer. Every education minister whether central or state would be looked down upon by the future generations when they would realize the extent of the damage caused by the haphazard and populist policies. Is there any wonder that people from earlier era, who were taught using now claimed as useless processes are much better than their equivalents? At least they had some basic understanding of their graduation subjects. There is also a question of hostility on the part of the listener. Such a mental state, never allows even the best communicators to say what they want to. For example, when Lord Krishna tried to negotiate for peace with Duryodhan, he could not succeed in spite being the best in the business. More recently in the debates between the ruling and opposition parties the hostility takes over and nothing worthwhile is achieved.

6. <u>Now if the sender</u> and the receiver are ready, the message becomes a problem. The message in form of a lecture, slogan, speech, write-up, advertisement and many other forms most of the times perennially fail to derive expected results. The designing of the message needs excellent command over language and today it is more than a trillion-dollar industry. However, when it comes to the efficacy of the message, we still are never sure about the same.

7. <u>The pronunciation</u> is yet another problem in the communication. When speaking, it is a major killer. Is it <u>tally</u> or <u>tele</u> in a telephone? Gesture, façade, gestation, genuine, 'skedule' and many such words are commonly not pronounced in a way they should be. What is right should be right. But it is not so!

The stylish accents may not work unless the words are said in a way they should be. Further the types of English add to confusion.

So, if we have to conclude we have to say that to regain the glory of language we have to seriously go back to grand old rules of language, learn them and more importantly use them while we communicate. No short cuts can help.

***

CHAPTER SEVEN

Corporate Acre of Diamonds

A very popular story in the HR circles is as follows:

During the famous diamond and gold rush, a person in South Africa wanted to try his luck in diamond prospecting. He sold his own land to whatever minimum price he could fetch and with that meagre capital ventured around the continent in search of a diamonds. He could not find any. He somehow continued. He somehow persisted for ten years, but then was very dejected, angry, and crest-fallen. At last, as a logical end of the circle, he reached his own town and out of curiosity he went back to see his own land.

The "land" no more resembled to what he had left like, but a huge manor stood on it, greatly imposing upon the surroundings. He asked the watchman about the owner. The owner, after purchasing the land, had found some stones which he used as paperweights. His friend, when he saw the stones, literally had a coronary attack as he recognized the diamonds. Upon his query the new owner said that similar stones were abundantly strayed on the land. This is how story of the start of Kimberly Diamond mines occurred in South Africa. The area is now classically known as Acre of Diamonds.

You would say 'Why this story now?'

The story is absolutely relevant in our lives. How often we abandon our land, our company, our employees, and start a new search in vain? How often we condemn what we have and try to find what we think others have? As said by Russell Herman Conwell the founder of Temple University we have to know that we are in fact standing right in the middle of our own customized 'Acres of Diamonds'. But we do not realize this simple fact. What we have is after all *proven, checked and tested*. It may not be as per our wishes but at least we have that much.

In the all-time classic Marathi drama, the above fact is dramatized beautifully. In the drama called "Tujhe Aahe Tujpashi", Pu. La. Deshpande, one of the greats of Marathi Literature, has put forth the facts of life, existentialism and pseudo spiritualism. It tells us what *we have now* is more important than what we think we can have in the future. Self- denial very rarely has answered any critical questions in the human life. Taking on the challenge is what is needed.

In any organization, of any size and volume, we are most likely to find the Acres of Diamonds. The question is what we do with it? Do we sit on it waiting for some miracle to happen? Do we really put our realistic efforts? Even if we find diamonds, we have to convert them from raw to finished stage.

On one side of the coin, where the diamonds (read employees) are available but the management usually uses them like paperweights. The management has rarely enough time, inclination, resources and most importantly the willpower required for the execution of the improvement plan. A diamond before cutting and polishing looks like any other stone. The diamonds need expert cutting, superlative polishing and proper settings to be able to fetch a proper price in the market is almost forgotten. The discussions are about the perceived *diamonds* in the other companies generally yield nothing great. Because of the no value assigned or low cost involved the diamonds in the company are very expendable. The talk of poor *input* quality is the mainstay of discussions over the sagging standards in education, industry, leadership and politics.

On the other side of the coin, the employees condemn the *land* (read organization)and set out to find the *new land* of opportunities.

They are dissatisfied, morose and behave similar to the lump of salt to be put in a pot full of milk. They spread the virus of inactivity and negativity faster than the *actual virus* could have ever done. They leave one organization to join some other and within no time find out that '*nothing*' really changes. In the new organization, once again they are supposed to *work*, *obey* the ridiculous orders and generally become unhappy. So, what changes? The quality of the employment is quite similar as it depends upon the similar socio-economic factors. Who becomes an employer and who remains an employee? It is *more* due to the socio-economic factors than the personal traits, in most cases. There would always be exceptions but they are far and few in between. Just enough to prove the rule.

Does it mean that you never look for change? Does it mean that when in the earlier century people worked in a single company or government throughout their lives overlooking the insults and other inconveniences was right? Does it also mean that earlier concept of *lifelong loyalty* is outdated? What is the last straw which decides that *enough is enough* and starts the collapse? The solution lies in the decision of a person and his limit of taking things lying down. There is no set of rules both for the individual and the organization and even if there is a set, it is always under the factor of correct implementation. The proportion of rationality in any decision rather than the subjectivity would decide the long-term impact on the person and the organization.

It really comes down to how you look at things? Is it a surface level look or the in-depth look? Does the sex, good looks, easy availability, favorable market conditions matter? How much Weightage is appreciated and in what proportion? Does the employee get enough time, space, and most importantly the needed support before he is ready to sustain the pain and get converted in to the diamond?

The company has to remember that the process of prospecting, mining, developing and processing the coarse diamonds is very expensive, painful and may be non productive and yet it has to continue with the same almost in a missionary spirit in accordance with the HR principles. The employees have to ensure that they are putting in great efforts to make their stay on the acre of diamonds productive and amicable. Once the diamonds start coming out, they both can rest assured of a continuous success.

***

CHAPTER EIGHT

IDEA

The relationship of an idea with any enterprise is very similar to the relationship an atom shares with the matter. Idea, at least today, is the smallest component of anything, that is subsequently termed as an achievement, very rarely gets the recognition it deserves. The original idea along with the original person with the idea is no exception, and most of the times are buried deep down the glare of the subsequent promotion and publicity.

The genesis of an idea is often very funny.

The double helical structure of the life particle DNA was an idea generated reportedly on a tissue paper in a coffee shop.

An apple fell down and the idea of gravity came into being.

Who can forget the first streaker, the great Archimedes and his legendary 'Eureka'?

Ideas have an unbiased attitude; they keep propping in the minds of all persons irrespective of intelligence, class, qualifications and ability. The difference in the idea fructified and idea aborted is mostly due to the persons *who got* the idea and what *they did* with it. What is more interesting is how many *new* ideas you would have to ignore so as to succeed with the present idea under the process. One of the major reasons for the failed ideas is the lack of discerning power in the minds of the persons who are in charge. The journey from an idea to a bustling enterprise is very arduous and exceptional. If we somehow can find out how many ideas were generated and never got to see light of the day, we may not still be able to calculate the cost and loss to the mankind. It is estimated that out of the total number of generated ideas only a fraction is working today.

They say that ideas have a strong bond with creativity in the humans. The relationship is directly proportional and often related with the free association of thoughts that the creative people specialize in. The 'no limits to thinking' principle is the first requisition for the generation of ideas. Whether the idea is prudent, feasible and actionable is of no concern and probably the last thing on the minds of the creative people. Smart management consultants have used this concept and designed the *brain storming* activity. Again, how effective it is for the clients is a debatable issue. It certainly helps the consultants as it gives 'a sense of participation' feeling to the paying client. What happens to the ideas, if any, after the session is a matter of research? Ideas and their generation cannot be compelled, which is often overlooked.

The concept of ideation is a peculiar. It is based on the principle of collaborative thinking. It assumes that when a group of people with similar intellect and interest is given a topic, the members would start producing thoughts. Irrelevant, or even out of focus, some also refer the same as rambling but soon after the process becomes more serious and focused. Even a single idea in a week generated in this fashion can be extremely productive. When one gets an idea and then he presents it to the group is the basic process of ideation. It is artificial and, in most cases, it works because management makes participation mandatory. The effort is worthwhile as it improves the group dynamics, if nothing else.

You should be prepared for any possible idea any time as it is very unpredictable. It always helps to carry a *small diary and to jot down* the idea, as even a faint pencil line is sharper than any memory. Moreover, it is permanent. Jot down your first impressions about the idea and the probable benefits it can accrue for you as well as the organization. Idea with right people can be very productive and the history is full of such examples. *Fate of an idea is bright if it gets associated with an optimist.* Due to inherent ability of finding positive side of anything he deals with new input in the form of an idea with full enthusiasm. Conversely a pessimist can wind up the possibility of any thing even before you can utter "Idea".

If an idea is in form of an opportunity, we tend to think about the very often repeated threadbare cliché: 'opportunity knocks but once'. It is probably one of the most wrongly represented statements. If this were a true statement we should not talk about ambition, initiative and inspiration. If idea is lost once, we should be lost forever, which is not the case, so ideas and the opportunities would keep on emerging and we need to be alert for spotting them. As manager we should know that ideas would always knock on our doors. The new products are in constant demand (the new product is a culmination of an idea). The companies are constantly looking for new ideas to be ahead of competition. A single idea is purchased for millions of rupees; new businesses are set up based on a single idea. Such businesses may need an idea rather than any specialized skills. So, a right idea in a right hand is what we are after.

As future managers you should be aware about the ideas, their generation and most importantly their proper application. A manager must realize that there is a time for the idea generation and the actual working. If this is mixed up the effect may be disastrous. A mere idea may not be always enough it is to be coupled with a determined person who is clear about the potential of the idea. The idea after being accepted has to be developed in to a concept. How it is done, we would look in to the same some other time. In the recent times a whole and comprehensive concept has come in the limelight, which is called Design Engineering. It is an integrated approach to the entire process of conception of an idea to the final commercial conversion in to something worthwhile product. The opportunities here are said to be worth in billions if not trillions of dollars.

The ideas die mostly due to what people say about its future. The usual words idea meets are impossible, unrealistic, stupid, impractical, useless, expensive, and many such expressions coming from the people who have never done anything original in their lives. such people are improved versions of bonded labors, the only difference is in the control. In the earlier case the landlord is the culprit and in the case of these pessimists they are bounded by their misconceptions.

A fantastic poem by Edgar A Guest described the negation in 1934.

Somebody said that it couldn't be done
But he with a chuckle replied
That "maybe it couldn't," but he would be one
Who wouldn't say so till he'd tried.
So he buckled right in with the trace of a grin
On his face. If he worried he hid it.
He started to sing as he tackled the thing
That couldn't be done, and he did it!
Somebody scoffed: "Oh, you'll never do that;
At least no one ever has done it;"
But he took off his coat and he took off his hat
And the first thing we knew he'd begun it.
With a lift of his chin and a bit of a grin,
Without any doubting or quiddit,
He started to sing as he tackled the thing
That couldn't be done, and he did it.
There are thousands to tell you it cannot be done,
There are thousands to prophesy failure,
There are thousands to point out to you one by one,
The dangers that wait to assail you.
But just buckle in with a bit of a grin,
Just take off your coat and go to it;
Just start in to sing as you tackle the thing
That "cannot be done," and you'll do it.

***

Visualization

You are blessed with an idea; you are sure about its potential, but not sure about the next step. Have patience, you just joined the majority. An idea in itself has to be lucky to originate in the mind of a person who takes some effort and works on it.

Human mind is equipped with quite a few specials; one of the most important is the ability to visualize. It is the formation of an image of something you have seen or what you would like to see in the future.

Let us understand the process.

Whenever and whatever a person sees forms an instant image in his mind. We say that we see with our eyes but it is a partially true statement. When we see an object, we are actually seeing it in our brain. The message from the eyes is interpreted here. How otherwise we explain the vividly colored dreams with our eyes closed and in pitch darkness? In that fraction of a second, many actions are taken at a frantic speed by our brain and it results in our seeing.

There is a big difference between seeing and visualizing. Some way similar to hearing and listening.

What we see and what we visualize are two different things. A *mere image* is not what we are talking about, but a complete picture full of colors, dimensions and other details and the future benefits possible from the idea in question.

It is a magic to paint the mental pictures. Some people cynically call it day-dreaming. They do not differentiate between the wishful thinking and aspirations. If mind can conceive an idea, it can become a reality, but only for those people who believe and persist. The people who are achievers are as a rule, dreamers. They are adept in *painting* mental pictures; *visualize* the future scenario and more importantly *see clearly* their roles in the picture. The trick is in *projecting yourself in the future* where your idea can be seen as a success. This single step creates a dynamic effect in the person. The pictures serve as a constant reminder and also as an inspiration. One thing is very easy to understand that you can choose to paint what you want to become. You can choose to paint yourself as a winner or a loser. Nothing costs you a penny and yet the effect is miraculous. The irony is that even though it is free of cost, most of excel in limiting what we see. We have to understand very clearly that if we can create our internal world, we have potential to change it.

Visualization forms a major component of the successful leadership. A leader sees what others do not see. What he sees as the future he converts in to images, fills colors in them, effectively shares with the people around him.

Many times, in the history this has been proved. The often-cited example is: In early sixties, President John F. Kennedy announced that America would put first man on the moon before 1970. It is reported that he just said it, without any back up information. When tackled by NASA, he said that he knew that they would do it. Nobody was sure as to how. The result, however, was that Neil Armstrong walked on the soil of moon in July 1969. Kennedy was no more, but what he visualized turned out true.

Most ideas meet a stiff resistance from the people. 'This is not possible and no body has done it before' is what people have to offer to any one, with a new idea. And yet we have so many inventions and discoveries, it is a tribute to all those who could see what others could not. Being a visionary is to be able to see the present and in addition correctly paint the future, including the idea one has. The visualization is comparable to a jig saw puzzle where in you begin with an idea of completing it. Some times it is completed in a flash while in some others, it may take even years to complete. *The point is that it always gets done.* The more the difficulties visualized, more is the pleasure of the subsequent accomplishment. Can you see the challenges, resistances, feasibility, chances of failures and success?

Yes?

You are on a right path. The fine tuning and the significant difference come in the form of an ability to see the solutions also. Solutions are the hopes. Where there is life there is hope and where there is a hope there is a better life. Where there is hope there is an ideal. Where there is an ideal there is progress. Where there is progress there is success.

The most important purpose served by visualization is that it enables the implanting of the idea in conscious and sub-conscious mind, setting correctly for the future stage of actual working on it. How idea can be converted in to an accomplishment is a matter of great interest and we shall discuss the same, in the Future. A person with an idea has to understand firmly that there is a great difference between day dreaming and visualization.

***

CHAPTER TEN

Promoting a Concept

In the journey from 'origin to success' an **idea** travels a lot. Travelling at the speed of mind and then at a reasonable speed of logic and feasibility. It speeds on highways, faces traffic jams, waits patiently for the rivers in spate of floods to subside, runs uphill and some times even runs out of fuel. The difficult part comes in the form of concept and its enunciation comparable to a dark tunnel on the road. The major difficulty is due to the fear of instant rejection from the people. The contest is not amongst the equals as the person with an idea is himself not very sure has to compete with the overbearing opposition, so sure of itself.

Idea is mostly in an amorphous form, which may or may not prove effective. Structuring an idea in a form acceptable to the people is the basic requirement of the conceptualization. **A concept can be defined as a mental representation of an idea (designed for future) which enables a person to describe, explain or in some cases even predict the way the proposed idea may work.**

It is always said that any project is done twice. The first time is when it is conceived in the mind of man with the vision and subsequently in the actual conditions when the idea is put to use. The picture which the man believes as realistic is his perceived version of reality. The perceived and the actual reality always coexist. We can say that there are always two aspects of the reality. The real one and what we perceive as the real one.

The first step in the process may be called as the verbalization. The person though sure about the veracity of his idea always has some apprehension before he verbalizes the same. It takes a great courage of conviction to talk about the idea to some one else. The moment one talks about the idea to someone else it becomes a public information. It is subjected to an appraisal. Fair or not so fair is the question which most of the people do not want to answer. Knowing, one thing is one thing and to express it, is altogether different. How you say it, is what the person has to learn and that too very fast.

The person has some reasons to believe that the idea (now promoted as a concept) would be successful. Can he say the same with some confidence? If the persons listening would be the financers, the stakes become heavier.

There are so many examples in the history which substantiate the point. Successful people any time in the history of mankind have an aversion to any new idea. The telephone, the radio was almost rejected as worthless. What a mess it would have been if the idealists would have given up?

Before presenting the concept to the world outside the owner of the idea has to convince himself beyond any shred of doubts that his idea is great and feasible. He must be a living demonstration of the future success.

The <u>proper presentation</u> of the concept can be the second step in the process. The presentation should be in line with the mental images the person had when he visualized the idea. The transfer of the contents should be able to generate the same levels of enthusiasm in the minds of the listeners. When the frequencies of both fractions match, a wholesome project is destined to initiate. It has been documented that the single most factor which is credited with the success of the promoting the concept is the **<u>enthusiasm level</u>** of the person who is presenting. The energy can not be faked at least as on today and hence it has a power to affect the people and draw a positive response.

Many worthwhile ideas could not see the light of the day as the bearer of the ideas lacked the necessary enthusiasm. Just like a successful farmer who carefully prepares his farm by proper ploughing, by removing weeds, and then only sows the selected seeds. To get a proper yield an optimal combination of all phases is must. After that the luck factor in the form of rains walks in. The process, the timing and the subsequent care ensures the yield. _That the idea in itself is good is never sufficient to be a success_. The conceptualized idea has to be put forth in a proper way, which leads it in the next stage of execution, which we would see in the future.

CHAPTER ELEVEN

Execution of an Idea.

You are blessed with an idea, have an ability to visualize the same in the future, to further present it as a feasible concept to people who matter, who can finance, and yet you may not be able to exploit the optimal potential of your idea.

Sounds not so great!

Why, you may ask me and you are most welcome.

The next phase, the execution, is all about doing, the action mode which actually converts an idea in to a success as in an event, as a smash hit in a movie, a tea making chain, or a Paytm, or as in the case of Café Coffee Day chain or on the other hand a routine flop film or a dead product. The trend setters are usually from a most unlikely background but what they lack in terms of material resources they supplement their efforts by belief, conviction and most importantly by their enthusiasm. The acknowledged success rate is less than 5%, which makes all the steps very vital.

All the earlier steps are, in fact, <u>sieves</u>. Each ensures that only a few worthwhile and feasible ideas pass through and rest is discarded. The matter is as it is very serious and it now needs a special attention to details. As you are the only one who has complete information about your idea you have to assume the total responsibility towards the success. Mind you I am talking of success. Onwards these points you cannot even afford to think about any possible failure.

The <u>first step</u> in the execution is to prepare a comprehensive action plan with practical deadlines.

The <u>second step</u> is correct sequencing of the events.

The <u>third step</u> is to find the people who are aligned to your thinking or at least those people who are not against you and your idea.

Some things are checked simultaneously. Such as:
- money for the execution,
- the check-ups,
- the stages of completion,
- the quality of the work completed,
- any corrective action on the feedback received,
- motivation of the members as and when needed
- maintaining discipline and integrity
- proper delegation of work load
- intermittent appreciation and rewards
- to ensure that the execution is as per the pre decided guide lines.

The above are in a random order and one has learnt to set each of them as per the specific requirement of the execution of a project in hand. The acumen of the person in charge can be a deciding factor in the successful execution of the project in hand.

The idea at this stage can be a product /service oriented or event oriented. Does it make any appreciable difference? Yes, to an extent, it does. Both activities need different sort of planning. The most noticeable is that the event management is guided by the deadline already set up by the organizers, meaning the date of the event is fixed, where as in the case of the product/ service execution some element of flexibility exists.

If the execution goes on smoothly from initiation to the conclusion, it is a certain rarity. The usual bottlenecks are always encountered and one has to foresee them and should have alternatives chalked put. Lack of funds on a continuous basis is the biggest culprit, closely followed by the slow speed of the contractors, the inexplicable government decisions, and transfer and quitting of competent staff. The principle of redundancy comes into play, however the cost incurred due to maintaining of such a state is a luxury very few can really afford.

When the things are not where they should be the perseverance of the man in charge is the only thing which offsets the resultant lethargy and brings back the project on the road to success. The sagging energy levels can be raised by a continuous impact of the man in charge. The de-motivated workers need a constant reassurance that they are still on the right path and that in spite of the current bottlenecks the success is just round the corner. Here, the true leadership of a person comes into forefront. The last few steps are always the most difficult, as has been said by the legendary Sir Edmund Hillary, the first, to set a foot on the Mount Everest.

Each idea and its execution are a case in itself. _There is no rule book, there is no SOP, no FAQs and no usual tricks._ One successful set of people in one execution team can never ever guarantee the success of an incoming new idea. Yes, they can be more likely to succeed. They have once travelled the less travelled road so they are aware of the potholes and rough patches.

So now, you have managed to set the idea in a form of a completed project or event. You should be proud and happy. However, a small bit of suggestion to you. Unless the entire process is duplicable (without any personal charisma), by any set of people, the idea may still not meet the expectations of profits. It is not enough to succeed once, but it the replication of the success module which makes an idea commercially viable. For example, the idea of Pretty Home Exhibition, which can be termed as a success and trend setter, as the organizers correctly duplicated the module in various cities and became almost a sort of habit to the people.

***

CHAPTER TWELVE

Image Management A Career with a bright Future.

Ever since people started to live in an organized society, the question of who is better and who is not has bothered the mankind. When a person is to be appraised by the people the right logic may or may not be a conspicuous part. Why a particular person is liked and disliked is a subjective evaluation and hence creates lots of problems. If the country is a democratic the chaos is much more. The freedom of speech, the right to information and many such things together makes the matter further worse. An image is what comes to your mind when a particular name of a person, place and process is uttered. Whether it is right or not is not the question. The question is what image you carry about them?

When we say Godrej, Bajaj, Reliance, Reserve Bank of India, Mercedes, Toyota, Opal, Haldiram some thing emerges in front of our eyes. The picture whatever it is the image of that particular name in our mind. It is neither right nor wrong. It is based on the information we have, and it is a very personal picture. It is called the **Image**. The image of a company or a person is a result of many focused and coordinated efforts of all stakeholders in the organization and their interactions with millions of people spread over decades. **Earlier, it was accepted that if you do a proper business, you would have a proper image**. To a certain extent it holds true even today. It is a slow process and results are more or less permanent.

The exposure in the past was limited; the media was not as strong as it is today so the workable balance was achieved. The reach was limited. Presently due to the information technology explosion it is very difficult and needs a concerted effort. There are dedicated teams who work round the clock and create an image or destroy the created image. In today's world it may not be possible for an organization or a person to depend solely on the performance. The relationship of what you do and what people think you do has become very complex.

The not so recent image management was in case of the President Nixon, whether successful or not is a matter of conjecture. How much he gained as regards the ratings and subsequent Watergate is again a well-known fact. What happened to 'Shining India' is a matter of common knowledge and hence the correct application of the image and its management is needed. The most recent campaign on the UP and the Crime can also be termed as a disaster. It created exactly opposite effect and flirted with failure. What went wrong?

The very strong campaigns against the central government whether in USA or India have been pretty successful and quite a few feel that the Trump Government lost due to a bad image management.

We can understand the same if we go in to the details about Image and its management.

Each organization has a certain image to begin with. Even before the organization is founded it inherits some image from its founders. Most people do not categorically differentiate between an identity and an image. Identity is a calculated, pre designed thing where as the image is gradually perceived by the people about an organization over a period of time. Identity can be controlled, where as controlling an image is very difficult if not impossible. So what is Image?

Say, in case of a purchase manager deciding to place an order for a product manufactured by many, when every thing is same in terms of quality, terms of payment, delivery schedule, the image the manager has about the company counts and that is what tilts the balance. Now, why he has favored a company over the other can not be properly explained even by him, as the tangible factors almost remain same. It is probably his feeling better dealing with that company. It is a subjective decision if I may say so, at the same time quite a few objective factors make him do so. The factor which makes him do so is the image and to make him think so is the image management. The people who specialize in this are called Image Consultants, which is an emerging trend in our country.

More often than not the consultants would be dealing with developing of the Corporate Image, maintaining the same over a period of time and consciously modifying the image as and when required. Corporate image is defined as the perceived sum of the entire organization inclusive of its products, employees, services, management style, their social responsibility and all such factors. The company carefully projects it self so as to influence the people for the best results.

Building a positive corporate image requires a skillful planning on long term and a comprehensive view of the total activities called as business. As against the specializations and the people going in for them, very trendy these days, the image consultant has to have a discerning and an all-round attitude. Even better put, he should have a 360` understanding. He should understand a significance of a small factor, which might be overlooked by others. He should understand, analyze and most importantly *exploit* the same.

The image consultants mainly work in two areas. They are:

1. Image of a person, such as an actor, player, professional, politician and even a head of a state.

Personal image consultancy mainly deals with the development of person on the inside and the outside. The image in terms of what he wears, how should he look, his diction, reading habits, oration and even some training in leadership skills. The next stage is a sustained projection of the person as an acceptable, able and model to the society.

1. Image of an organization, such as a company, a political party, a family empire, an NGO, a government department a bank and so on and so forth.

As against the personal image dealing with the organization is not as easy as it involves many diverse activities and persona. We would dwell slightly more on this aspect. The ideal aim of a consultant is to finally create a cohesive global image of the organization in question in a reasonable time frame. So the consultants look in to each and every aspect of what is called as business.

The major activities can be developing an image from the inception stage or redefining or refining the not so good present-day image of the client. The areas which are very important are as follows:

- The name
- The mission statements
- The products and positioning
- The brand equity
- Customer perception
- Staffing and HR policy
- Promotional policy, activities, their sustained effects on the perception
- The sales and more importantly the after sales service
- To be able to fight the set backs: even the companies with a long standing can find a whirl wind. The recent examples are the Cadbury, the Coke. And today, Nokia. What matters is that they have regained the balance.
- Managing the correct ratio of referrals

- And many such activities.

To explain my point, I would just talk about the proper names. There are certain accepted norms of how a name should be selected.

When Daewoo decided to launch in the States, it ran a campaign with a punch line 'You know who, Daewoo'. The effect was totally misplaced; people remembered it as a 'you know who company' rather than Daewoo.

Irish Mist, a company with some repute had to stop marketing its liquor brand in Germany as mist in German means 'manure'.

So, there is a lot to a name, however if to be discussed it would need a special treatise. there are consultants who specialize in the naming of a company.

As already has been mentioned to be an image consultant one has to have some relevant experience in business and its management, the theories and the current updates, practical intelligence and most importantly the required set of human skills. This is a career which should ideally start at slightly latter date; however, some exceptional persons can begin their careers as image consultants. They would need some guidance which is always available for the deserving.

***

CHAPTER THIRTEEN

In Search of Excellence

Do you know any normal human being who <u>does not want to excel</u>?

The answer to this rarely asked question ideally should be a plain No. If I further ask you to name a few persons around you, who have excelled in their respective fields, you would again find it difficult. Why should this happen? Every one wants to excel and yet very few ultimately do so. This does not seem to gel. Are there enough books, journals, people who give enough information on how to excel in any given field? The answer is yes; there is probably no other subject, on which so much has been said, written and researched. So many thinkers through out the world are trying for so many centuries to find what it takes to excel and how the same can be transferred to the willing human beings. In spite of all this effort, it would be still a bold statement to say that the mankind knows how to excel. Can every one really or hypothetically achieve the excellence? The answer is 'yes and no'. Not that we do not want people to excel or we think that people are not gifted enough. Each person when born has a potential to excel. All the coaching classes, academies never say this publicly, but deep down they know that only a few (of the admitted) have the potential and are able to deliver when it really matters. Let us try to find out what is the matter with people and excellence.

So, is it something to do with the genes? If it were so then only a few would be born with the entitlement to excellence. It would also mean that the fate of children born to ordinary people is sealed right at the stage of their birth. Thankfully, it is not so, most of the very excellent achievers had very ordinary parental input.

Is it something to do with the circumstances in which the person lives? Again, thankfully it is found that the adversities were the motivators to most of the excellent achievers. Eklavya, Chandragupta, Madam Curie, Alexander Fleming, Dhirubhai Ambani, Eknath Solkar, Kapil Dev, Dr. B.R. Ambedkar are some of the names which are at the top of my mind but we can find so many others. What was the common thing in all of these great human beings? The answer to this question by each person can provide a very wide base for excellence, and yet you would probably further confuse your thinking.

Coming to the younger generation who should be the real beneficiaries, from such an effort, should remember one thing that they all are good. The question is whether their goodness is enough? Excellence is always in comparison, so it is relative. What is good for one set of people may be a starting point for the others. What is good for us may be worthless for some others. The parameters are different, set of people re different and hence the excellence also differs.

Let us talk about the competitive exams, which are the acknowledged litmus tests for the excellence? Are they really comprehensive? Can they really assure the excellence in a person once he passes the exam? May be not, as the exams are touching only one point of life, which is academics. Being good in academics alone may not be a key to excellence. Clearing such exams cannot assure excellence; otherwise, how can we explain the state of our country, which is ruled by the so-called excellent people who clear the top civil exams. So, something else is needed along with the academics.

What is then excellence?

Let us define:

Excellence is **defined** as doing one's personal best, while striving to go beyond it.

Excellence can be again divided in various parts. The two most important which touch our lives daily are all round excellence and specific excellence involving the subject matter or any skill.

The other aspect about the excellence is the consistency with which one is able to deliver with same intensity and quality. It is a matter of common knowledge that mere presence of even top most quality of talent may not deliver excellence. The examples of Kambli and Tendulkar or Yograj and Kapil Dev are very typical. It is said that the first one in both pairs was more talented but in the long run could not deliver. They may have their valid reasons but then reasons can never replace the results.

So, if young person decides today that he wants to achieve excellence what should he do?

The first thing to do is to write down the specification of excellence. What he wants to do, where and in what time frame? It should be remembered that the goals should be slightly improbable but not impossible. Writing down of what you want to achieve is the first concrete step towards the excellence. It creates a right focus and attitude. However, the percentage of decline at this stage itself is phenomenal; very few believe in themselves and hence avoid writing.

The second aspect which decides the ultimate success is the right choice of the process and the choice of a person supervising. The usual *'chalta-hai'* supervision has *destroyed* many potential excellences. Excellence means 'the best', hence cannot have any tolerances.

The third thing one has to be always conscious is whether or not he is sticking to the right process irrespective of the initial setbacks. That, how one tackles the setbacks, is one big factor which decides whether one would achieve the excellence or not. To fall is natural, to cry after he falls is also natural, but it takes a great strength to rise after the fall. Those who manage to rise and complete the race are the ones who may achieve the excellence.

The key to excellence also lies in the fact in the continuous evaluation and subsequent up gradation. You should always ask yourself on a daily basis: "Am I better than yesterday?" when your mind answers 'yes' you should try to analyze why and also that whether or not you can continue with what made you better.

One more question which is very relevant in student life is "Is this my best effort?" Nine out of ten times your mind would tell you 'No, you can do better' so before any submissions, exams, interviews, and assignments, this question needs an honest answer from the purest effort. Find out what three improvements you can incorporate, edit your contents and you would be at least sure about your efforts.

It also helps if you can find out any person in your circle who you think could have done a better job. Find out why and again apply the changes which may open one more door for the excellence.

Lastly it is imperative to find out for whom you want to excel? If you are able to dedicate the excellence to some one very near and dear to you it tends to keep you on track and gives you that extra bit to excel.

So, go out and excel yourself in the field of your choice. Never settle for any thing less. Wish you all good ones for an excellent future.

***

CHAPTER FOURTEEN

The Leadership:

Can we coach somebody in to leadership?

How much time would it take to produce a leader out of an ordinary person?

If leaders can be created why there is a dearth of leaders across the country and even globally?

The experiments of leadership conversions are abundantly available in India. By now, I am sure that you have recalled at least ten names ranging from sons, nephews, grandsons, daughters and wives of local sundry corporator to the prime minister. The success ratio is questionable. The logic offered is that if it can happen in the business and professional hierarchy, then why not in the sphere of political leadership? By the time the "leaders" are ready (if at all) the precious time is lost and the nation is on the back foot most of the time.

The classical leadership is mostly inborn (as in case of Shivaji Maharaj or Samrat Chandragupta) and not forced or acquired as in many other cases. That by common sense and practice one can become a leader is possible, but that is very slow and tedious. The original leadership and the acquired leadership can be as different as chalk and cheese. The acquired leadership though not impossible is generally very improbable and even if it happens the cost involved is beyond normal comprehensions.

Very often it is observed in our country is the case of "reluctant" leadership. Almost all Indian Prime Ministers fall in to this category barring a few. When the person is forced in to leadership, he finds himself there at the top without any struggle, so he can very rarely value the position at the top. He has not gone through the grind so he is not conditioned; or pretreated and hence is not as tough as required. India has suffered immensely and opportunity costs are running in to trillions of rupees. To start as a lowly member of party cadre and rise through sheer grit and commitment evolves the true leaders.

Take a case of a typical leadership in Indian Business Family. The original first-generation entrepreneur was successful because he had a dream, and he then decided to chase his dream. He had a single-minded laser beam focused approach and he never got diverted. He in fact never thought about all such things. He just worked day in day out, slogged, begged, borrowed and probably sometimes even stole. His successors generally are not as single minded and hence do not get similar scale of success.

The current situation in our country has probably raised the above questions in the minds of the people.

Do we have leaders or not?

We feel that we are very close to be politically orphaned. The society on the whole and the role of leaders in it, both are under a microscopic scrutiny and the results so far seen are not very encouraging to say the least. Further depression arises from the fact even most of youngsters are falling in the age-old trap of corruption, nepotism, lack of integrity, and most seriously lack of national outlook.

We are discussing a question of imparting the leadership education. Can someone really be taught to be a leader? Can there be a safe and proven module of teaching or training aids which can produce leaders and somehow guarantee their performance? Leadership is extremely complicated issue with innumerable variables and very few of us have any real understanding about the process or its development as well as control. Others have tried the time-tested methods of 'support the rising star' and wait for him or her to develop in the leader. There are advertisements which claim to teach the leadership; more often than not they turn out to be mere hot air. In the last 60 years we have true leaders who can be counted on the fingertips. This is in spite of so many management institutions, career's counseling, so much free flow of information, so much technical development, so many favorable situations and probably a better literacy rate. The point that is always missed by all such people is that the leadership is a function of thinking in a different way while doing a routine thing, that too on a continuous productive scale. What they further miss is that a leader in one situation may not be so in other. The much-cited example of Sir Winston Churchill signifies the point. He was a darling of all Englishmen during the War but was removed from the helm of affairs the moment the war ended. That means that the leadership also deals with expertise needed to resolve a particular issue.

The question is where do we look for the leaders? Are we going to import them? Or in even more modern terms can we *outsource* them? And if they can be outsourced what about our own variety! The outsourced would replace whom?

Or do we simply depend on what the Lord Krishna has said in 'Bhagvad Geeta' that wherever and whenever anarchy occurs, whenever the culture and religion is stupefied, He dawns an incarnation and saves all of us.

Whichever way we look at it we come to realize that very soon something is destined to give way and some extremely drastic steps would be necessary to restore our sense of well-being and retrace our path of glory.

***

CHAPTER FIFTEEN

Loser's Limp

There is a game going on in the mind of each participant in all sorts of competitions, which forms an interesting part of life.

<u>Every one begins with a win in mind.</u>

Nobody wants to lose and yet at the end of each 'race' there is only one winner. The winner wins and the rest lose. If this is accepted, life would be very simple, but we do not lead a simple life. We know so many simple things, which would make our life a great saga of success, but very rarely we pay attention to our inner voice. We neglect what is obvious and end up trying to find excuses for our failures.

I read about 'the loser's limp' in 'See you at the Top', a book by Zig Zigler. When I analyzed, I found that many of us are having temporary or chronic attacks of the loser's limp. When it comes to improvement, most of us 'delay' instead of 'do'. Anyone who has competed in sports knows a thing or two about 'loser's limp'.

"<u>Today we have a generation of men who suffer from 'loser's limp'</u>." says Tony Evans in his book "<u>No More Excuses</u>".

Loser's limp, is something you do when in spite your best efforts you know that you would not manage to win or finish. For example, a fielder chasing a ball realizes that the ball would beat him to the fence, suddenly pulls his leg and just to put up a brave face to the crowd, some how ambles after the ball, half expecting the people to say 'Oh! God! He would have saved the four, but for the cramp'. May be, the crowd has genuinely believed the bluff, but what about the player himself? He knows that he has pulled a farce; he would have any way not saved the runs. But doing what he did, he has not only managed to save 'face' in front of his fans, but to a certain degree has managed to cheat his own inner self. At least he thinks so. So many people do the similar things in life. They keep pouring out the reasons for their poor results.

The fact remains that he has simply failed.

Let us dwell a little more on this attitude. Why we need to justify our failures? Why there is such a hue and cry over failures? Why so many reviews, meetings? What do these review meetings really achieve? Recently, for the first time since the modern Olympics started, India could not qualify for Hockey in the coming Olympics. What followed was a big comedy. Every one was vociferous about how the earlier management should be kicked out. Subsequently, it was changed. Has it really changed the lots of the hockey players? They still travel by railways and that too in second class, minus A/c. Even today they use outdated sports gears, still practice on grounds without astroturfs. They still have no fan following and still if they lose any more; the people would find reasons not with administration but with players only.

Losing is an operational mistake, meaning even if you lose you still have to play a full game. Mistakes are also same. Unless you do something, you cannot err. The people who do not attempt do not achieve any thing unless they are politician's progeny. In our country it is regular that a son or daughter is accepted as a winner not because either has proved any thing but because of the earlier generated parental pull. What is the result we all know; yet we cannot change the limping democratic norm.

The reasons for 'not doing' are a part and parcel of the loser's limp. The loser waits for the right equipment, right time, right people, right environment and conveniently forgets that some one else is achieving great things with same resources. We are in a 'too much analysis leads to paralysis phase' and so the result is a foregone conclusion. He, our competitor, wins and we once again start giving reasons. I remember that one of my *khadoos* bosses had a readymade list of excuses, prominently displayed on his table. He used to acknowledge any new reason and add the same to the list. After some time, we could not manufacture any more reasons and started working without bothering for failures, the percentage of success improved. When we do not have losing on our minds we generally win.

So, the best policy about doing anything successfully is to learn to leap instead of worrying about the proverbial limp.

CHAPTER SIXTEEN

The Man in the Mirror

Man is the only animal who has understood the significance of the mirror.

Without a mirror we cannot even see ourselves. The first introduction to ourselves, as to how we are, is possible only because of the mirrors. The first time we see ourselves in the mirror we are thankfully devoid of any baggage's, which we accumulate later in our lives when we are supposedly growing mature. We usually like what we see. That is simply because we do not have anybody else to tell us whether we are up to the mark or not. Later when we are examined, tested, evaluated, and finally appraised we see the dark part of our lives, they say mirrors do not lie and they say right.

Who can forget the funfairs and *melas*, where the mirror houses gave us the pure joy of looking at ourselves and the lighter moments? The mere joy of watching our forms in concave and convex mirrors was simply great.

Mirrors are the friends of the man right from the ancient times they have helped us to look better. We spend some time before the mirror every day depending upon the so many factors. The time spent in front of the mirror has also something to do with the gender, it is commonly accepted that the fairer ones spend more time than their counterparts. A lady, in one such discussions said very 'tongue in cheek way' "It is but natural that we spend more time in front of a mirror. We do have many things to watch. We have to *watch*, to watch that more people *watch* us." Very true and no arguments over this! A mirror is arguably responsible for the proper presentation of 50% population of the world.

Somehow our relationship with mirror becomes less significant as we supposedly grow. We tend to take things for granted. We think we know ourselves. We forget what we are capable of and what we have done. We forget the preparations we had in front of a mirror just before we stepped in the professional life. We start looking for the solutions elsewhere. We forget the old buddy who has helped us in many situations. We forget the man in the mirror who is our best friend.

When you see in the mirror you instantly know whether you like what you see or not, when you do not like what you see you start think in extreme situations which make you feel that you are the loneliest person in the world, you realize that *the honest man in the mirror* is still with you showing your strengths and weaknesses. The point is whether you have the right kind of perception and whether you understand what he is trying to say.

The man in the mirror can be your conscience, your self esteem, your potential and most of the times your performance which could have been much better. The mirror has an uncanny knack of telling you the truth without any possible embarrassment. Any other person whether your wife, parents, teachers very rarely can achieve telling you that you are wrong without causing a pinch of anger and embarrassment.

At the beginning of your careers, you want to do many things and do them in as best way as possible. What you want to do is not always supplemented by the required knowledge, talent and skills. You want to achieve the best with not so best resources. As a result, most of the times you meet with a stiff resistance, ridicule and no support, which further adds to the difficulty levels. The good news is you still want to do the best. If you have any doubts try to find out a person who does not want to be successful and happy. Try to find a person who plans for being unhappy in the day. Every body wants to be happy and yet at the end of the day very rarely turns out to be a happy person. In such a situation the man in the mirror can be your best friend.

When you get up in the morning and start for the daily routine you invariably are in front of the mirror. Tell the man what are your plans for the day, what is the minimum you are certain to achieve and further what problems you may face. While you are at it the man starts telling you what is good for you and what is not. The more the intent in this activity better are the results.

When you get ready for the day, just before getting out of your homes once again you are in front of the mirror, which tells you whether you are up to it, in terms of what you are wearing, are they in 'sync.' with what you doing. Please listen to the man. If he tells you that your clothes are not ok, do change them to suit the day. Pay some attention for the simple reason that if you do not like what you are very few on the outside are going to love you. While doing so, rehearse the whole day's schedule in front of the man in the mirror. When you come back home in the evening, sincerely report your activities to the man in the mirror, you would find the routine very soothing and also that your performance tends to improve. The rehearsals you do polish your performances, they increase the chances of a sustained success levels. The improvements that are certified by the man in the mirror add to your inner strengths and you start to enjoy the work you do. To enjoy what you do is the first concrete step towards success.

The best part of the process is that no body else knows about your efforts and reasons for the recent successes. Once you are branded as a potential success you would find that your life changes and you move in the fast lane of life.

***

CHAPTER SEVENTEEN

Management Education: Today

One of the most sought-after careers in our country today is the Management Education. Not surprisingly, most students want join the league. They join and start behaving very peculiarly. With the result, very few become managers at the end of the 2 years. What they at the most become is a negligible MBA. The curriculum though very comprehensively designed, does not really help and where curriculum promises potential, the delivery usually fails.

Management as a curriculum is extremely vast. It spans from the elementary mathematics and English to the concepts from engineering, systems, projects, accounts, costing, finance, human resources and to top it all, the intriguing world of marketing. <u>It is not easy.</u> The students need a specific aptitude, which is not tested at all in the age-old entrance tests carried out by the States. The person needs to be clever even to understand that the course is integrated. He needs to perceive the 360° scope and application of what ever he can learn in the stipulated time of two years. The superficial smartness, if we can call it so, which is intentionally imparted by the immature teachers to the aspiring managers makes things more difficult. MBA to most means a plush job, flying in and out of the country, every thing at least 5Stars, a decent office and staff who is supposed to be working their hearts out for the boss-who else but the manager?

Presently most management students can not define management even in their final terms of courses. They do not know anything about Henry Fayol or Peter Drucker, very rarely they have ever touched Kotler's book on marketing, they do not know any thing about managerial skills or to put it mildly they do not know what they do not know. They expect to be a manager and their preparations are for a job of a salesman. Most of them can not speak or write the language 'English'- properly. Many cannot even read it. To top it most teachers very conveniently tell their students that English is not necessary to be a good manager. Reasons are obvious for doing so. The teachers themselves are horrible in English. This is a statement so bad that it almost equates blasphemy. An aspiring manager MUST note that no person *at least in our country* can become a manager without English. He should maintain a safe distance from any such person who tells him that English is not required in management.

In the first year or the semester a subject called as 'principles of management' is taught. Nobody takes it seriously, neither the teachers nor the students. This is one topic which actually unifies the diverse student's fraternity, orients them to learn all other related subjects. The concepts of MBO, POSLC, motivation, standardization and many such frequently used terms are overlooked by the students and teachers. The initial confusion leads to a permanent cobweb and the student comes out as confused entity. The transition from the spoon-fed graduation levels to the post graduate application-oriented courses never ever takes place. The students are aware that the management education is more about application of learning rather than plain learning. The prevalent, probably most used and hyped practice today is to teach the students to form hypotheses from class learning's. Further, they supposedly gather, analyze, interpret the data and then review their hypotheses in light of their findings. It has been shown that such prediction-investigation-interpretation-reporting cycles are crucial to correct common misconceptions by students. In short, the teacher can contribute about 35 to 40 percent; the rest is to be acquired by each student by his or her personal efforts. The teaching methodology is a tool, which cuts two ways. The application of the concept looks extremely impressive on the paper but to effectively implement, the total commitment required is missing in teachers and the students. No teacher can ever teach or predict the experiences of the individual student when he starts to interact with the outside world. It may be for the surveys, research, actual selling, primary data collection or the consultation with experts. The process is very ambiguous and the student has to be extremely alert to pick up the bits or the pearls of knowledge. The reading habits are to be inculcated, nurtured and matured again by the students themselves. The language as well as prevailing jargon is to be internalized by the students as we have yet to find out a way of spoon feeding the same. The availability of information at the finger tips, the vast reach possible because of the internet, the dissolving of national boundaries, very strong possibility of network and yet it is felt that somehow the potential is not rightly tapped. Very few students actually use the net and its immense potential to the fullest. The concept of development of the vision is needed and the ability to visualize is to be taught. A student who can see what he can achieve in the future is the one who reaches there.

The process of the delivery of the knowledge is more pompous. Meaning usage of the presentation aids, power points, lesson plans, academic delivery schedules and feedbacks can not replace the contents and experience of the teachers from the field, which in most colleges' non existent. There are no 'qualified teachers', which means, that there are qualifications, but no teachers. The management which runs the college is greatly responsible for such a situation. What is said is 'Yeh saal chala lo na boss, next year we would employ good teachers.' As if next year some magic would create new superfine teachers!

With the globalization, privatization and liberation of education policy has created more *confusion than clarity*. This privatization has its negative impact also. Student is acting as market force. Student is the power while faculty is weak in these private institutions.

Indeed, the faculty lacks the position, expertise, and autonomy as they traditionally enjoyed at universities. Basically, they are supposed to serve the students and their practical orientations in commercial private institutions. These institutions rely on part-time faculty. When employing full-time faculty, they pay meager salary. Perhaps many of them have neither practical nor academic expertise and lack training. With these resources the claims of placements have to be met. It naturally creates conflict. But in standard institutes the 'intellectual capital development' is one of the main key results areas for the faculty. This helps a great deal. Even the freshest faculty some how puts in efforts for the continuous self-upgradation, under the guidance of the seniors, which is any way the essence of the profession called as teaching. The students from such institutions are more down to earth, more dependable, if not brilliant. The students respect such teachers and the result is visibly better as compared to the mushroom management institutes.

Another main focus in the modern management education is the case studies approach. Again, it is easier said than done. Very few can actually dissect the case; further few can really put the case in the proper perspective of the management curriculum. But if the matching is achieved this is the best method to understand the application of theory in practice. The cases, the case lets, the published papers, the current news on the topic in question are to be seriously scrutinized for effective delivery in the class.

Most teachers forget that the students are to be elevated in stages through their two years stay in the institute, which means that the teachers should be able to raise his delivery standards during this time. The students are good to note the difference and are extra alert in such a class. In the first semester the teacher has to coax and cajole the students for a proper induction and in the latter parts of the two years has to raise the bar for a desirable management student.

The industry interface is the vital factor in the completion of management education. What a teacher can explain in hours can be delivered by the industry manager in minutes and the students take it as a gospel truth.

To conclude every management education stake holder has to be very watchful must look in retrospective, about each aspect to be delivered to the student. Similarly, the student should stretch to maximum levels, absorb every bit of information to excel in the non forgiving business world. When these two would work in tandem the MBA would regain its lost glory. So let us look for good managers in the Future!

***

CHAPTER EIGHTEEN

Management learnings: A paradigm shift

We were discussing the correct and incorrect ways of teaching and the learnings from the same. When this topic was initiated by one of my friends, the first thing that I realized was that it is 40 years since I first learnt any thing about the management. I say 'first learnt' as my education is still very much on and I wish that it ideally should never end. The wonderful memories of my teachers are as fresh as if yesterday and I remember with immense gratitude their efforts, expertise and ability to transfer the knowledge to even students like me. So, is there any difference in the management education, method of teaching and testing, if yes, can we really find out whether it is moving in a right direction?

We were taught in a classical 'one to many' lecture mode and the time was 90 minutes per session. The teachers were a mix of exceptionally good and average. The first could cast a spell and any topic could be interesting. The fluency, the command over subject, ability to quote from the vast experience, the wit, the ready references and the excellent analyses of the current issues with respect to the topic taught was strictly from the top drawer. There were no OHPs, LCDs, not even a white board and yet their sessions were pure magic. The average really had a hard time to keep up in the competition, some how they barely managed to explain the topic, minus the magic. Now, majority of teachers can not teach unless aided by the slides.

There is one more basic difference which deals with the scope of respective subjects. Marketing for us was a subject with chapters on retail, distribution, advertising and others. Now each chapter has grown in to a full-fledged specialization (*referred to as an elective*), which is good. Details always help, provided your basics are at right place.

The prevalent, probably most used and hyped practice today is to teach the students to form hypotheses from class learnings. Further, they supposedly gather, analyze, interpret the data and then review their hypotheses in light of their findings. It has been shown that such prediction-investigation-interpretation-reporting cycles are crucial to correct common misconceptions by students. The approach is very much based on the premise that both students and the teachers **know** what they are doing and are **committed** enough to meet the required deadlines. More over the universities following this practice should have lesser stress on the classroom teachings. How many of our management institutes follow this approach and if they do, what is the correctness? Saying and actually doing are two vastly different things.

Our generation is very lucky, fortunate to witness so many changes in practically every field, technology, information flow, the over all speed of life, the ease of life, the sophistication at least in the material side of the life. Although we are zapped by these changes, many of us find difficult to grasp the full potential of the available advances at our fingertips. Today we are experiencing economic growth, at a frantic pace, yet many of us feel insecure about their jobs. Indeed, there are no more "safe" careers. Job security is almost a thing of past. However, it also has created a basic side effect. We are witnessing a definite fall in the standards, what is now called as a commodity work culture. Such workers are dime a dozen and create a stiff competition to the otherwise deserving people, not ready to work for peanuts. While inevitable technological changes challenge our current ethical, social, moral, administrative and economic systems, we as management teachers have to ask ourselves whether or not we are preparing our students to cope up with the required level of excellence with a great speed. I feel that any talent should be suitably rewarded and that can be possible only when a working balance is achieved between the original talent and the Xerox copies.

The proliferation of sub-standard management institutes across the country is probably one of the most potent dangers to the actual performance at the work places. Due to financial compulsions to some how run the institutes, the quality of the students is greatly compromised and yet at the end they get the same qualification. Further, a spoon-feeding culture is propagated, which may sometimes give somewhat impressive short-term results but in the future, it results in the spoiling of one complete generation. It is ridiculous at the present level and unless some drastic corrective actions are taken the sanctity of the whole education process becomes very doubtful. The stress therefore has shifted from a mere selection of the candidates to an elaborate selection process and yet the HR people are facing an acute shortage of people even for the commodity work class. The present generation is smart, but the smartness ruefully lasts mostly for only first fifteen minutes. The polish starts eroding as soon as the need of details is stressed. The sophistication available is to be used as the supplement rather than as a replacement of actual hard work.

The availability of information at the finger tips, the vast reach possible because of the internet, the dissolving of national boundaries, very strong possibility of network and yet it is felt that somehow the potential is not rightly tapped. The concept of development of the vision is needed and the ability to visualize is to be taught. A student who can see where he can be in the future is generally the one who reaches there. What else can a teacher possibly want more than a wide spectrum and dispersal of his successful students across the globe?

The teachers in the fields of management must strike a balance between the teaching aids and procedures. Mainly, they have to understand the limitations of PowerPoints, charts and graphs. The main component of the teaching even today should be a hardcore subject matter. If the teachers are dependent on the PowerPoints, for delivery they have missed the entire point of teaching to an adult.

It is very difficult to compare any two eras in any activity, the effort is made so as to derive benefits from the experience and use the enthusiasm of the younger generation to translate the experience with the help of a cohesive effort culminating into a resounding success for our country.

***

CHAPTER NINETEEN

Managing Success!

Volumes have been written over how to be successful, more successful and achieving success even when you are presently a failure. To most of us the success as and when it comes, *is arguably* a stroke of luck. May be, one who is successful does use the conditions slightly better than the others. I have no objection to becoming successful; in fact, I believe that it should be the sole and principal objective of our existence. Presently, we would try to see what one should do when he is successful.

The biggest exercise of becoming successful is prevalent all over the world. Some people are successful by design but most of us are there by default. The chances of having lasting success are much better for the first category. Mark the word '**chances**! Even the people who reach their goals by design may not necessarily know how to have continuous glory. For example, the people who top the merit lists in their earlier life are not always where they could have been. Does it mean that they could not manage their success? Does it mean that they slogged without understanding the concepts? Does it also mean that they mugged up every thing and just mechanically reproduced or even worse just acted as a virtual Xerox machine? The machine gives you an 'exact' replica of the original document, but certainly *does not understand a single alphabet* of the document.

When the success principles are applied to the popularly termed as 'the corporate' the picture is even dicier. The situation is more or less similar whether in the small or the medium or the largest, the success may be is dependent mostly on the topical factors such as a favorable government policy, a convenient connection in the high places or as in most cases plainly luck. In Indian scenario, very few have been able to succeed without any government influence. The induction effect of the government or political influence is responsible for the rise and fall of the business. For example, the CCD. It flourished almost unnaturally under the umbrella of political influence and when it was removed, it resulted in a tragic end. Talk to any person who is working in an acknowledged successful organization and you would know what I am talking about. Can he really and truthfully say that his organization is riding the success wave which was pre-designed? What is the special effort that goes in keeping the success?

When a person or an organization is climbing the path of success, there is very little time to look back and for a review. During this time many people who are not as good as they should be are somehow tolerated. The organization during this time neither has time nor inclination to spend any extra time in proper selections. The stress starts to show when the orders start pouring in and there are very few people to whom the organization can look up to. In such cases most organizations try the dangerous path of offering incentives to the *existing unfit* employees, which sends a completely wrong signal to the existing employees. Incentives and their subsequent ad-hoc disbursements are the two largest factors which threaten the continued success of the companies.

Mostly, people tend to take Success very lightly, whether it is a person, an organization or even the nation. We have seen many students placed in the coveted merit list doing nothing spectacular in the future lives. We have seen what happened to campaigns like "India shining" or "Garibi hatao". Very few really understand how success has come or the correct process responsible for success.

Most organizations that were successful just a while ago are now fighting for their breath in the turbulent waters. They tend to forget one simple thing. The duck looks very calm and serene on the top of the placid water, but the constant pedaling under the water is not seen by the people. You stop the pedaling and the trouble sets in. The success is like the mountain weather, when it is nice, it is incomparable. Within next few minutes the scene changes. The crystal-clear sunshine is gone so much so that we start asking whether we really saw it. The rains, the winds and other hazards make every one miserable. Similarly, when the organization is successful, it looks good. Every body looks happy trying to create an impression that he is wholly or at least partially responsible for the present pleasant state of affairs. The media runs the interviews of the top people who somehow always appear wonderstruck with the unexpected results. When the boss says that his organization has excellent man power he remembers all those who have been pain for him. When he talks about sound financial position, he recollects the calls from his bankers. When he says they want to expand, it usually means that they are about to be kicked out of the presently operative areas. Such successes remind me of that bucket which in spite of many holes some how gets full and then the drain starts.

The management of success hence is as important if not more than being successful. If the success is a product of one spike zone in the graph of the performance, then more often than not it would have a small life. So, measuring the routine functions and ensuring that the day-to-day operations are efficiently monitored can result in a stable success.

Many of us equate success with growth. Bigger size may or may not be a result of success. If not managed properly the adage which says 'the bigger they are, harder they fall' fits in. Take a case of Satyam, it was big, so, it fell big making a crackling noise. The stock exchange scams, the Telagi stamp scam, the fodder scam, all were huge and grossly mismanaged.

Success has a sort of lulling effect on the people or the stake holders as now a day called. They are sure that the success is in spite of their short comings and hence in the future also they would get the success. It is here the seams start bursting. May be one or two times the system had the inherent capacity to balance the upsets, but that is not any guarantee for the continuous success.

Success also generates an unwanted race. About 'who' is right rather than 'what' is right. The organizations going after 'who' generally fail very fast, as their system is person dependent than process. Correct Process is the key to the success. Correctness at planning of the process and its subsequent appropriate implementation, independent of the persons handling the process can be a suitable basis for a continuous success.

Success needs to be bound by a predefined set of parameters. Volume, penetration, distribution, profitability, employee contributions, flexibility, ability to diversify, ability to duplicate the success models, expansions over the continents, exports, earning per share, and many such aspects. If there is a variation it needs to be handled with patience and the process needs to be crystallized so that when the same variation occurs again the organization knows what is to be done. Success is more likely to stay on course if the company is more process driven than person driven.

Success which originates from an innovative idea may be is smaller as compared to success which is due correct duplication of that particular idea. Commercially, more duplication generates more money, power and stability. Take an example of Macdonald's, the key to their lasting success is due to their ability to multiply their successful model across the world. Whether USA, China or Russia they serve the same menu with minimum or no variations at all. Moreover, they are aware of all the problems, pitfalls in the model and effectively ensure that they are better prepared to face the problems as and when they arise. Any new variant if confronted is added to the list of the problems.

We have to look into one aspect very carefully. What is usually assumed is because we are successful so far, we would continue to succeed in the future. In this we tend to overlook one simple principle: Life is dynamic and, in its dynamism, it has potential to provide more opportunities as well as problems. Competition, changes in technology, changes in political systems, international money policy, disgruntled employees, dissatisfied customers, material shortages and many such factors are to be correctly tackled if one has to manage the present success. The popular term being 'proactive' looks very good but can *be extremely counterproductive* if not understood properly. One more aspect which decides whether you are managing success properly or not is your sense of timing. They say that an invasion of army can be stopped but not the idea whose time has come. The tapes vs. CDs, cable TV vs. the DTH, can be some relevant examples. The new things once accepted by the society sound a 'go away alarm' for the older ones which get replaced.

Lastly, we all have to seriously know the fact that says 'what goes up comes down'. The art of mastering the dives can be the difference between a chance success and a sustained success. The organizations can learn a thing or two from the Olympic divers. The key to the success is to delay the coming down, sustain the present-day success levels and be extremely alert to avoid any shocks due to ignorance, accidents, strikes, overall changes, marketing myopia and inner dissatisfaction both on a personal as well as the organizational levels.

Marketing myopia tops the list of reasons for a failure in the industry. Many were sucked in the intense whirlwind of stagnation where they sincerely believed that what was right for decades would be right for the future decades. The tastes of the consumers or the customers these days are guided by the very powerful almost wicked media, so what is good today can never see the light of tomorrow. What is suggested is to maintain the spirit of the entrepreneur even when the business is roaring like a lion. In cricket terms your form is as good as your score in the last innings. So, diversification, innovation, product improvement, design, understanding the competition, world scenario and international dynamics need a constant effort and reviews.

When the organization is successful it may not feel necessary to find the reasons for the same and that is first trap. Someone somewhere in the hierarchy has to be awake and he must constantly check for the warning signals, check them and initiate corrective measures.

***

• 75 •

Matter of Grey

The season of placements is almost over in most of the professional colleges and the long-awaited important phase of the 'generation next' is due for the onset. Some students are knocked out in the literal sense as they have somehow got the jobs. They are taking it easy and very soon would find it extremely hot, when they start working in the famous Indian summer, both literally and physically. Some of the prudent ones were curious about what they would do when they are placed, they kept on asking questions about how to tackle the transition in to an employee, so this article is for those who want to be successful in their chosen careers.

The difference in the approach between a green inexperienced and a grey mature person can be a main reason whether a particular person achieves noticeable success in the material world of management or turns out as a mediocre variety. The matter of grey is to be understood very neatly if one has to avoid the black failure. What one may see and what one may not in the initial parts of his career can turn out as 'the' factor to his success.

As a young green person, that too with a fashionable management degree of MBA, you tend to find in the early part of your opted career that the there is much more to the management apart from the classical theory. The mere application of what you are supposed to have learnt in the Institute rarely leads to the glory. The understanding of the management concepts whether in finance, marketing or the human resources is certainly needed and yet you find that unless a proper matching of the relevant concept with the arising situation is achieved, you may be groping in the dark. The difference is rarely in what you know, but more often in what you do not know. The further question is if you know something what you do about it, how neatly you do what you do. Moreover, it is not enough that you do something once in a while, what matters is how consistently you do it. Management is doing right things at right times and ensuring that whatever you do is duplicable, meaning somebody else apart from you is able to duplicate the results, under your leadership.

So, as an aspirant manager it helps if you begin right. You should be very clear that even after you pass out and get a placement, in most cases you *may not still know what you do not know*. The first step is to consciously put an effort to find out what you do not know about the management concepts. Go back to basics, study the basic chapters and ensure that you know at least them in the best possible way. Understand one thing, from now on you study for yourself and your career prospects. The biggest exam is beckoning you. The life is an exam and it never is over, unless the beats finally stop. So is your education, it ideally should never stop.

The management is all about problems, challenges and their solutions. Welcome the problems. Do not run away from them. Remember that it is only because of problems faced by the employers, they need you. *If there are no problems you are not needed at all.* The problems have to be solved and the challenges have to be overcome. The problems are very rarely pure white or black. So, the solutions accordingly have to be sought. The random combination of white and black generates an infinite grey area of problems, having innumerable shades of grey, indicating the various degrees of seriousness of the problems. To overcome such situations day in and day out you need a lot of grey matter and more importantly the willingness to properly use it.

The grey matter is supposedly in direct proportion with the grey hair one has. I think this may be not always right. The intelligence, which comes from the grey matter, has nothing to do with age. <u>You must remember this.</u> You are young and are blessed with abundant energy, which may form the ideal replacement of the experience. With each solution you create your personal experience and that is your personal property. People may rob you of every thing you may possess but so far nobody has managed to rob any one of his experiences.

I know that you are capable of achieving the highest glories. I always feel "You are the best! Do you know it?"

So, enter the world with your heads high and make us proud.
***

CHAPTER TWENTY-ONE

Options

Man is blessed with power of thinking. It helps him to choose, select and opt for the best of the available options. At least this is what the theory says!

Most of *us opt for the things*, which we would not have, if things were in our control. Ask people why they are doing what they are and very rarely you get logical explanations. You are surprised when you find out that a person is what he is today is not necessarily he had planned for. He further tells you that the present occupation was his third or fourth choice. He would also tell you that due to some factors in his past he had to opt for a career he is in. What is more intriguing is that most of such people are doing pretty decent job of what they doing today. So much for the right choices!

With what options we are sent in the world? We do not have option of choosing our place, time, family, status, health or for that matter even sex. How many of us keep on saying that but for this 'xyz' reason I would have been very successful. How many of us waste irreplaceable time in whining about things, which any way out of our control? The mentality of what we cannot do rather than what we can do emerges out as the single largest factor for the overall non-performance observed in our society.

Whether it is the matter of opting for the jobs, career, place of stay or spouse very few can really say that they have got what they opted for. I know such a person who became a doctor because he wanted to be, subsequently opted for then unknown as well as unheard of specialization. Today, he is one of the best in the field not only in India but all over the world. Was it easy for him? No, not at all! He slogged for long hours, underwent a hell of ridicule before he won an acceptance and acknowledgement personally and professionally. Today he can recline and smile about it. The reason is very simple. This is what he wanted and he has got it. The example is cited because I feel that he had the guts to opt for what he thought was best and then actually make it happen. Most people do exactly opposite. They decide for the moon and then do not do anything, subsequently settling for the ground floor they are staying. Lowering down the bar is the easiest thing and most often done.

It is a matter of common knowledge that most of sales targets are achieved in the last week of the month. What happens during that time is yet to be fathomed and in spite of a lot of effort, the last week can not be created in the first or second week of the month. The persons, the products, the processes and even the possibilities are more or less same yet all of the above cannot combine to produce the desired results in the second week. Why? The answer to this frequently asked question is yet to found out.

Most students study only at the end of the academic session just before the exam, most people start regular exercise only after warned by the doctors, most people repay loans when it is overdue, most people some how adjust to their married life, only when they realize that no further options are available. This is a very serious issue and needs a specific handling. All such people rue over lack of options when it mattered. If it is possible to go back in the TIME and once again offer the same situation, I feel that most of them would choose the same as they have done in the past.

So, what to do? Accept what comes our way or weigh critically each available choice, then select the best with respect to the present conditions and hope for the best. The best way to deal with options is:

1. Be thankful for the options and think about those who do not have them.
2. Learn to do an instant Cost Benefit Analysis and project the same in the future.

1. You realize that only one of the options can be worked with. So, learn to calculate the opportunity costs of each overlooked option.
2. More choices generally confuse more.
3. Your actual *"do" phase* starts after you opt for a choice. <u>All options need someserious</u> working.

It is classically said that people do some thing not because it is the best option but mostly because it is the last option. It is a matter which requires our immediate attention and may be coupled with some remedial action so that we not rue over our options in the Future.

***

CHAPTER TWENTY-TWO

Performance

<u>All</u> that matters in a man's life is his performance in various stages of his life. What he does in a day as well in the night matters. He knows it and he should be ideally trying to improve his performance in each of the vital areas in his life. Some men are successful, some are even more successful, some keep trying to be successful and some never get any where near the accepted level of performance. Most people are afraid of the appraisals. The bosses who are responsible for the evaluations review the performance, the deviations from the accepted levels and then decide about the raises in the salary or the promotions.

The performance in education, employment/ or profession representing the financial aspect, as a family man and as a part of a large social structure together creates a successful man. Any missing component ruins the taste of success in the remaining fields. Success of any person, in an isolated area of evaluation generally not as acceptable as the overall success of the person, it tends to analyze rather than appreciate. Moreover, the person himself does not seem to enjoy the limited success. He rues, he always remembers the areas in which he could not be as successful.

How can one ensure a sustained performance which would be measured against a pre-decided set of parameters? Parameters are quantity, quality, value and a time frame. In a material world any thing that can not be measured has very little practical value. They also say that what cannot be measured does not grow. How much, at what quality, what is the incoming revenue and is it in the prescribed time frame are the four pillars which support the performance palace. You take out any one of the above four and a justification for a short fall is warranted. In addition, performing once is not just enough and has to be repeated on a continuous basis.

One who performs consistently usually has following traits. He is confident, focused, cheerful, sure about his data, he knows the correct process, he is ready to try some thing new, he knows that he can initially fail, he is ready to ask for a counsel, he is patient, he can appreciate the success and the difficulties faced by others, he has a plan for every day and most importantly he has the belief that he would succeed. When things are not going the way, they were supposed to go he can stop for a while, reassess the situation and most importantly regroup for the yet another try at the target.

Some people perform once and then they find that they have lost the touch. Performance is one thing which is not automatic or guaranteed. That you were successful once does not mean that you would be always so. Each attempt at each new or the same task requires same effort levels; though it may seem easy as you know how to do the task from your previous experience.

Performing for self and getting somebody else to perform are two different things. An operating manger when promoted confronts this challenge when promoted to supervising managerial position. He knows how to but has no clue about to get the things done. Now, the qualities like patience and readiness to get a counsel usually help him in learning to supervise and manage. The key to be a good supervisor is to remember that people rarely listen to what you say, but certainly see what you do. If you do what you ask them to do usually you would turn out a good performer at both levels.

Those who appraise the performance should remember to isolate the peaks and spikes found in a time frame. What matters, is whether in given and normal circumstances the person is producing results. The spikes represent a windfall or seasonal performance and in the long run have a tendency to fade away. It should be taken as a bonus for the sustained effort rather than depending on the spikes for the next performance. The objectivity in the appraisals is the key to a sustained performance of the organization in the years to come.

The method which is prevalent is to put pressure. It may be in the form of coercion, threats, abusing and shouting. This is a method that may work temporarily but once the junior decides that 'enough is enough' no amount of bulldozing can produce desired results. Most people believe that fear is the key. Maybe it is so! But then the key would be functional till the fear exists.

The performance resulting from an inner will tends to be more satisfying than the one achieved due to compulsion. The satisfaction is very visible and can be in most cases contagious. When a non performer stays with a performer, he tends to learn the tricks faster and starts performing. The performances most of the times come from a passion rather than pressure so it pays to be passionate love what you do and if possible, do what you love.

When you do what you love to do you are bound to perform better. But in the rational world you are rarely in such a happy situation. The real performer is who performs in every thing he does whether he likes or dislikes. The magnanimity arises from the equanimity. The intensity of the effort is not dependent on the preferences. He performs irrespective of the situations, oppositions, opportunities or absence of them.

When you start doing some thing, be sure that there would be mistakes. Remember that one who does not make mistakes usually does not do any thing worthwhile. There would be trials, failures, frictions, betrayals and even then, you would be successful if you have the passion to sail over the depressing times. What seems very smooth today was very turbulent a few days ago. Just like a duck, it looks inactive and peaceful on the top of water but there is an incessant peddling under the water to keep it on the top.

What ultimately matters and what you remember is that you are a performer, that you are successful. When you yourself do not remember the problems you faced, be sure that the world would never do. So, decide what you want to do, start doing, as a mere thought and inactive person have never achieved anything worthwhile.

***

CHAPTER TWENTY-THREE

Presentation Skills, Fears, etc.

We know thatpresentations are vital for advancement of any professional career. We gather knowledge about this fascinating activity from various sources and make ourselves aware of the recent trends. I feel that mere accumulation of all such information has a limited use, unless practiced properly. You may not agree and you are in majority.

When person enrolls for swimming, he is taught about the breathing techniques, various strokes, *outside the pool.* everything seems easy! He is motivated enough to venture near the swimming pool and then even dives. *After that moment, his world changes for ever.* All lessons in the theory prove inadequate; he finds that he is going under water and when even his voice deserts him he is terrified. The depth of the tank, the presence of the coach becomes irrelevant and the pure fear rules his mind. Once outside he is panting and puffing, fighting to breathe as if it is one last time, totally disoriented, cursing the coach and vowing never to venture anywhere near water. AND yet after a few weeks, the same person is invariably enjoying the joy of diving, underwater swimming and most importantly encouraging some new person to overcome the fear.

This is one great lesson of life and is very comparable with a person about to undertake presentation for the first time. He has been taught, coached, coaxed to step on the stage. He does so and then he is never the same person again. It does not matter whether he is successful or not, he has learnt a fundamental lesson in his life. He now knows that he is very alone when on stage. The fear of talking to public is second only to the fear of death and to overcome you have to just do what you are afraid of.

The presentation is divided in three major parts.

1. The **preparation** is a part of presentation about which you can be sure. You have loads of information, you choose what you think is relevant for the topic and the would-be audience. The presentation is a step towards understanding hence needs to be solution oriented. If you discuss only problems, you would find that the audience is more knowledgeable. The preparation should be the exact description of the problem and your approach to the solution. In fact, the problems are one of the most basic reasons for holding the presentations.

Following points should be at the top of the mind of the presenter.

- Check the title. Is it magnetic enough?
- Check the contents, their authenticity and accuracy.
- Check the power point presentations. If you are using the functions like hyper link, pen drive or action buttons you should be doubly sure that they work.
- Use appropriate graphics as they explain much better than the mere monotony of the voice.
- Follow the basics of the Power Point presentation, such as the a) uniformity in the background, b) fonts, c) animations etc.
- Pictures are preferred over words.
- Stories are a very refreshing aid. Third party effect is very well received. TPE means that you not the only one who is wise, but someone else. You are delivering the message.
- Time bound sub-sections of the presentations always help to retain the interest of the audience.

- Be sure to rehearse. The mirror can be your friend as it never lies and what it tells does not embarrass you in public.

1. The **actual presentation** is usually for a short time unless you are engaging a day long session. *This essay is not meant for them*.

- The first thing you notice when you reach the site is the **ambience.** The correct judgment here is vital for any further success as you can fine tune your presentation.
- **Use emotions**. Emotions are real. They make the presentations more interesting.
- **Appearances** matter a lot. You ensure that you appear cheerful, happy, sincere and if possible intelligent.

- **Converse, don't perform**. Nobody can listen as a group. **One listens only for himself.** Talk to each of them. Address individuals in the audience. Look them in the eye, and then look at the next one. They should feel that you are talking to each one of them. Like in a temple, there are many devotees but each feels that the god is looking at him and even talking to him. Minus the god part, everything fits for the presenter.
- **Use first and second person voices.** Presentation is about 'me and you'. Not other people.

- **Command the space.** The stage is yours. Move around. Don't stay behind the podium, if there is one. Step out into the open, where you can talk freely with your audience. Get into a place where you can see the screen as well as they can. Left side of the screen is the best option. (Usually, 45 degrees angle is ideal.)

- **Stand to the left of the screen.** People read left to right. They should start with you and move to the screen.

- **Break the flow.** In the middle of your talk, turn off the screen (if you can) and interact with the audience.

- **Watch yourself**. It's shocking to see yourself on tape. It is really shocking but there's no better lesson than the ones you learn by watching yourself and learning form your mistakes.

- **Edit aggressively**. Less said is more permanent and clearer in the minds of the audience. So have a ruthless approach towards the unnecessary details.
- **Relax**. It's only a presentation. *There is always another time.*

The Feedback and follow-up- It is relatively easy but very vital as it brings you more money, recognition, clients. A smart presenter knows that he has to retain all his enthusiasm for this stage. How best you can create the data base and further use it for the generation of the business is decided at this stage. The feedback helps you to improve as it is coming from those who have suffered/ or enjoyed at your hands. It is suggested that this activity must be manned by the best in the organization to maximize the yield.

The basic thing that makes a presentation exclusive is though it is thoroughly rehearsed it should give an impression of spontaneity. You may lose the number of the retakes but for the audience it is always the first time. At last, what you must remember is "You may know everything; your presentation is first class and yet when you climb on the stage you would be tense. You would not be normal. What you have to realize that your being "not normal" is in fact a very normal routine, just like the person in the swimming pool.

You would learn and relish presentations in the near future. The happiness after a proper presentation is almost ecstatic. If it fetches an order or a promotion it is like a cherry on the cake. So, be ready for the accolades! They are overdue!

***

CHAPTER TWENTY-FOUR

Sense of Belonging.

Out of the entire animal kingdom only humans have to be especially motivated, so much so, that these days it has turned into a huge industry. Humans, with powers of thinking, talking, discussing and progressively developing intelligence have only *partially* succeeded in reaping the benefits of these endowments of God. The vital reason for this lapse is that we lack the sense of belonging. If you ask any HR person in industry, he would say the same. If you do not know such person, then you may ask yourself whether you *belong to the place you work for*? You would be surprised to know what your mind tells you.

In the recent past entire world suffered very gravely and almost came down on knees in front of the Covid 19. Again, the humans suffered more than the animals. The total concept of the existence was questioned. So many suffered, so many died and yet somehow the spark of the humanity was also bright enough. When we know that the weight of the entire virus that shook the basic foundation of human existence was less than ten grams, we came to know how fickle we are in front of the Almighty. The bond between the organizations and the employees was put to its ultimate test in the two trying and testing years.

What Alvin Toffler had predicted in his now a classic book, Future Shock, regarding the relationships of the employees and the companies has come true. The changes are remarkable.

There is a remarkable difference between the performances of the persons who belong and who do not. The *extra input,* which is inadvertently put forth by the people in the first category, distinguishes them from the others. The tragedy in the last six decades of our independent existence lies in the fact that we have not inculcated this feeling in our employees, businessmen, students, bureaucrats and the Politians.

The moment people *feel that they belong* to the organization they work for *they are different people.* They work better, treat their clients better and most importantly they begin to feel better. For example, I would like to share my experience, while I was in Kolkata for training in one of my companies. We traveled in the Metro, and were very impressed with cleanliness at the stations. The fact that the cleanliness was limited to the undergrounds only, was puzzling us. The outside Kolkata was as dirty as it always was. We discussed this in our meeting and our director, a staunch Kolkatan, told us that it was probably because every citizen felt that the Metro belonged to him and hence kept it clean just like his own house. Remember nothing else changed. The city was same, the public was same with same education levels, but somewhere inside their hearts something stirred positively, to produce the unbelievable results.

The value of such a change is never easy to calculate but it reflects in the balance sheet of the organization in form of *added profit and better dividends. Most people work very hard to get a job, but afterwards they hardly work.* They while away time and because they do not work, they spoil others in the time they otherwise would have spent in working for the organization. They pride at themselves, feeling that they have very smartly cheated their respective bosses, but they never realize that they are cheating themselves.

What changes occur within a person as soon as he is confirmed in the service is a topic of research. The security of a permanent job instead of extracting the best out the person tends to lull him in a false sense of security, and the result is degradation in the quality of the work output. Sadly, this is true in both public and private sectors, though in different scales.

The HR people in most organizations apparently work overtime to get their people to belong to the organization; however, the success rate is towards minimal. This can be traced back to the times when the persons concerned joined the organization. The root cause can be never really pinpointed; however, there could be a diverse set of reasons, which cause a serious damage to the organization. *The cost in the terms of wasted opportunity is intangible.* If all persons in a company feel that they work for their own company, can put in a terrific synergistic effort, which is anyway possible only in humans. The extra stretching in terms of an added effort that they otherwise would have never tried becomes possible only if they feel that they belong to the company.

In the present-day scenario, they say that the working environment is not conducive to put in a sincere effort. One is lured in to the devilish ring of corruption, and finds one or the other way of avoiding what he should do. Sadly, in the government departments in India, he is briefed by his colleagues that the pay he gets *is just for attending* office, and any work he is supposed to do should be done only if he gets the bribe. Such a person can never belong anywhere, neither to his organization nor to his nation. The lack of integrity disables him to put his best effort. He sadly misses the gratitude towards his employer; never realizing that his family is *well to do* because of the salary his employer is giving. Whenever, such a predicament arises he should simply go back to the first day of his joining and recall the pleasure, the confidence, and even the status, he had derived from it. He may subsequently change the jobs but even then, only one player has changed, rest everything remains constant.

Discharging duty correctly gives an immense and irreplaceable pleasure. It adds fulfillment to life and gives better self-esteem. Every evening you should be able to tell yourself that you are eating your dinner after a sincere effort at your office. If you can do so over a period of time then you would find a new meaning in your life. In the arrogance of youth, one may not understand the value of this, but as one grows old the realization dawns that he has wasted a beautiful opportunity called life.

***

CHAPTER TWENTY-FIVE

The event and the eventuality.

The activity is in a full swing!

Everyone is busy or trying to look busy!

You suddenly see some people who appear, as if, by magic and dominate the proceedings whether or not welcome by the real worker bees.

Some of the smart Alecs are stressing the need of their expertise, how people do not have senses, how the last event failed and how the same set of people are again ruining the present one. There are many who have personal scores to settle, their own axes to grind, they have scant respect for the event and try every thing possible to increase the difficulty levels to maximum. Their agenda is simple; they want to have a last laugh, so they wait to see the result of their underhand deals.

I know when you read this; a flash-back of quite a few events would unfold in front of your mind screen. Let me further say that very few changes have occurred since and the proverbial fight is still on. *The doers in any event and the leg- pullers are as old as Adam and Eve.*

The positive thing is that, despite all these odds, the events are arranged and they are successful, which should give some solace to the future organizers and event managers.

Is there any way to learn the event management? What a question? So many institutes claim that they do exactly the same.

They run the courses on the event management and at least outwardly give an impression that they have the expertise to do the same. With huge data available, people are lured in to a sense of a false security. It appears so simple and organized when you read the articles and further when you see the colorful shining photographs as the testimony, you are ready to launch yourself as the event manager/ coordinator.

The time between 'today' and the date of the event is the key factor. Do you feel that you have sufficient time to plan and further implement the plan? In most professional organizations this is looked into very seriously and this may be one reason why their events are mostly meeting with desired success. When it comes to the other type, the chaos starts from the date itself. It is a matter of hours rather than days here and it creates immense stress, confusion, ego clashes, and verbal fights, which in worse cases can turn into the physical versions.

In most cases an organizing committee is formed and with this simple step the seams in the organization become visible. How a committee is constituted can be of great significance; is it through a democratic or an autocratic process, can decide the success of the aspired event. What is the face of the committee? Does it represent the brains or just beauties? What is the acceptance rating of the members? It is seen that a nominated committee has very little chance as far as the success is concerned.

Next step is the inevitable meetings, some productive others not so. Planning, coordination, preview, review are some the common names of the meetings. The meetings are for the advancement of the purpose, rarely it seems so. Unless a very strong and focused person is at the helm of the affairs these meets can turn in to a big waste of time, as well as in to a blame game. There is usual quota of tantrums, tears, torn papers, thrashed egos and trampled persons.

With all this preparation, if we may call it so, the D Day dawns and the pressures are at their peaks. The Chief Guest has just informed his inability to 'grace' the occasion, the caterer's mother has been admitted to hospital; the compeer has a sore throat, the accountant has just now declared temporary bankruptcy, the number of the participants is declining to a critical level, the delayed start is coinciding with the load shedding of electricity board, some body could not get the necessary government permissions, though reportedly the event has been okayed verbally...... It seems that it just goes on and on. The poor person in charge is at his wits end and there is a queue of persons demanding instant decisions. <u>What he does now is the Event management in practical conditions.</u>

Madam Ayn Rand in her epic novel 'Atlas Shrugged' has said that when in doubt, check the premises. This may prove as the guiding principle for the event organizer. He has to have a basic belief which has to be constant in spite of the pressures and pains. He has to have a facade which emits strength and optimism. This is easier said than done, but good thing about it is that it can be achieved through practice. The first time is bad but it improves with each attempt. Each additional try can at last give him a sort of his own personal event management manual which is much better than just theory. The theory is important as it is the starting point and because of the same reason it also has its limitations. I have my own share of events and their managements so obviously I have my own key which I am sharing with you all, I hope the next time you organize any event you would have the success as expected.

1. The first thing is the correct scheduling of the date of the event.
2. You find out the people in your organization, who are like you, think like you; find out all those who are at least not against the idea.
3. The action plans are to be made with the allocation of purpose and the proper persons. No compromise here is a good policy.
4. The check lists of the activities to be ready by a particular day are a must. Ideally '7 days before, 3 days before and 24 hours before' checklists serve the purpose.
5. Planning for the D Day.

a. Segmentation of the entire event in 15 /30 /60 minutes segments helps you to keep a proper control.
b. The segment coordinators should be given authority and unless some thing foolish is not done they should not be over driven.
c. The scripting of the events is a must. The rule here is without a pre checked script no body goes to the stage.
d. Strong yet courteous people for crowd control are needed.

6. Some basic things are to be reminded to all who matter. Things like the ambience and the decorum of the event, no arguments with any one for any reasons or provocations. Avoid arguments as they can kill the event, even if you win an argument, you are more likely to lose the event. The only priority is the event.
7. "This is my event and I would not let any person to ruin it" is the guiding principle of the event manager.

Ask yourself why some events are successful and others are not.
Go back in your memory lane. Remember the events where you felt like you were a part of the event, where you felt that the operations are moving ahead in a cohesive effort, where people organizing believed in what they were doing, where the event coordinator had a casual dominance and yet he was courteous, where credit was not mongered and you would set yourself in a proper frame of mind to launch the event. What you should never forget is that you have to retain the same spirit till the event is concluded and applauded as a success. All the best for the Future!

***

CHAPTER TWENTY-SIX

The Magic Wand in Manager's Hand

During my association with what is now popularly addressed to as 'The Corporate World', I have learnt many and unlearnt many things. Many old concepts are still valid while quite a few have been replaced with more contemporary ideas. The process continues today and probably would do so for the years to come. People talk of management in their daily routine and expect all others to understand what they say along with straight and oblique references. However, it is felt that very few have a clear-cut idea about the management and the real potential of this wonderful process.

- Why do we need any type of management?
- What is the real process?
- Do we believe in the management process?
- Or we keep on saying about the practical situations, and limit ourselves to first available compromise.
- What we have presently as management science, is it really sufficient for the fulfilling the needs of the ever-expanding needs of the business and the organizations?
- What are the daily inputs for upgrading the existing systems? Most importantly, do we **feel** that we know enough of the management process through its basic components of **planning, organizing, staffing, leading** as well as the **control**, and then

only we promote the same? If everything is so well planned, organized and further implemented, **why** things go wrong?

The answer to this WHY is probably the "real" management.

Wise men have said that the management is more of common sense and its correct application. The problem faced today by almost all organizations is the shortage of common sense. <u>Proper profit, supported by the properly motivated employees, in a properly maintained business environment, is almost a myth</u>. The spokesmen in organizations do not want to elaborate on this sour point, but in private conversations it is an openly accepted fact. If everything is done after so much planning why it should go wrong, why people should find time to play the blame game? What is the status of the organization when its employees, who are supposed to protect its interests, fly on ego trips? The surface level talks of the priority, integrity, loyalty, teamwork, and sharing remain only at the surface. The matter of survival takes over everything else and as a result only self-promotion remains afloat. One of the worst things that has hit the Indian scene is the increase of hollow and shallow people who do not have what it takes to succeed by work. So instead of some honest efforts they stoop down to lowest levels and start the internal politics and spoiling the team. Such organizations despite of their sizes, hallowed positions generally are doomed. We know many organizations, political parties, institutions, in our vicinity who have stopped to exist. To understand this chronic problem, we have to look in to several aspects of business and its management very seriously. Business is finally an activity to be done on a daily basis and by all stakeholders in a synergistic way or else end is never too far away.

The business is selling a product or service either in a mix or in isolation, to one or many customers, creating a profit over a period of time. It is very simple if we keep it simple. To keep things simple is not simple. The problem faced by most flourishing businesses is that many times the **business almost assumes a human form and starts behaving as if it has its own life.** It is called as a nearly irreversible process of getting dictated by the circumstances. The management even if desperately desirous of gaining control cannot do so. The situations, which are impossible to be simulated, really test the operating managers and in such situations, the knowledge and the basic belief in the system are the only friends of the managers.

A common man with very mediocre abilities can over a period of time and after a lot of practice may acquire expertise and succeed in the same. Why? Because he somehow manages it well. However, a manager has to achieve his goals keeping in mind the interests of his men, their limitations, motivating them under strict guidelines of pre- decided profits. This he has to do year after year with acceptable levels of success and it is here the dilemma originates. The dilemma is **management for man** or **man for management**. Each person has to find his own answer for this often-posed question, and no one is wrong.

The word management should be studied in a little more details. Classically, management in early seventeenth century was an act of managing or manipulating. (Surprisingly, *manus* in Latin means hand.) Moreover, it was in the context of training the horses. If we extend the line of thinking, we may split the word as Man+ age + ment. The first part the man is the most vital as without man nothing matters. More likely we are concerned with the man who is coming of age. The man who is maturing or ripening is more suitable for the process. Ment is the part of mentoring. So, Management can be helping a person to grow, mature by proper mentoring.

Managers have to remember for his life that the magic is rare. The correct execution on a daily basis may create a magic. the ability to repeat the mundane and boring tasks is no less than a magic.

So, what is Management? Achieving the pre-decided goals with available resources over an extended period is management. **Watch for two words**. The first is **"pre-decided"** and the second is **"available"** resources. A manager cannot wait for ideal package of resources or for ideal time, because such a thing never exists. He has to be a resourceful person and has to manage with whatever he has at the present time. He remembers that the wand by itself has no magic and unless he pulls some trick the magic fails. There comes his magic and he only knows how to waive his magic wand to produce results from the proverbial hat.

***

CHAPTER TWENTY-SEVEN

Why employees do not work?

A very direct and uncomfortable question 'Why employees do not work as they should?' is probably the most circulated and discussed question in the HR Circles. Some HR people try to find the answer and spend their entire active lives, may even submit a Ph.D. and yet may not provide satisfactory answers.

The terms like the ones listed below
work ethics,
work culture,
work study,
motivation,
training,
incentives,
rewards,
awards,
organizational traditions,
monotony,
appraisals,
increments,
attitude,
aptitude,
ability,
value additions,
teamwork

and many others,

which have been literally ruminated over for years and yet if an employee is not working there is very little the management can do.

I have to implore you to recall situations where application of HR principles has resulted in a transformation of a non performer in to a performing asset. There would be some such instances but they would be few. I have my own share of the woes and I wish to share my impressions with knowledgeable professionals like you all.

There is a famous sentence that people work very hard to get a job and then hardly ever work. Twenty years on an average is what one puts in for acquiring the qualifications. These days sadly all qualifications are made available to the students at minimum efforts levels. Qualification without corresponding level of competence is the major reason for all problems arising in the future. What you get practically free does not instill any sense of pride. It results in a very low self esteem. We know that a person with a low esteem is a serious candidate for inefficiency. He can not be a team member or an achiever.

Let us try to find out more about this scenario.

1. The first thing the stake holders in the process have to realize that no person joins an organization for not working or performing. The feelings of the employee on his first day in the office are never negative. He wants to prove that he is competent and willing to work. He is ideally full of enthusiasm and seriously believes in the organization. Whether he is able to retain this frame of mind in the longer run is the question we all have to address. What are the factors responsible for his conversion in to a success or a failure? What is the contribution of the individual and of course the organization? Is his supervisor able to correctly remind him First day in the office and for how long?

1. The employee many times does not simply know what he is supposed to do. Here the training activity comes in the fore.

The training should give him a clear picture about what he is supposed to do, what is the correct process, the acceptable time frame is which he is supposed to do, what should he look forward to as and when he completes the job at an acceptable way.

3. During his initial working in the organization the employee finds that his salary is lesser as compared most of the people whom he thinks as inferior to him. This single fact is the biggest factor and must be one of the conspicuous reasons for most non performers.

4. The employee does not work properly if the promises in the interview are not fulfilled. Very few senior managers remember what they promised the prospective candidate in his final selection interview. Once forgotten is forgotten for ever. The dissatisfaction germinates here.

5. The job profile and the actual job assigned many times do not match resulting in the non performance.

6. One of the most cited reasons is the inefficient boss. The boss ideally should be **Better Organized Superior Soul**. Translated simply it means that if the employee is not able to do a certain task the boss should be able to do it in a better way. In our country most bosses seriously believe in bulldozing their way out. So long as the employee can bear this attitude, he some how manages to do his job, but presented with the first chance he revolts.

7. In government sector the selection of a candidate depends on many factors and corruption tops the list. The candidate here gets the job not because he deserves, but because he has literally bought it. Why should he work? He is more interested in recovering the money spent. Most employees here are just for

the attendance or for looking up for an easy grab of money.

8. In the software industry the basis of billing to clients is cited as one reason why some people have no work. The billing pattern is based on per employee per hour basis. Overstaffing is the rule which works in the favor of the non performers.

9. The change in technology works as a major factor for the non working of employees. Recently in the public sector banks when the computerized banking system was introduced many of the earlier better employees could not keep pace with the change. They could not work.

10. The change of the product lines affects the working. Again, when the public sector banks entered the Insurance sector, they simply transferred their earlier employees to the insurance activity. That it failed was a foregone conclusion. A person selling some thing and a person doing a back-office job need different mindsets. No inspiration coupled with name's sake training can result in dissatisfaction and resultant failure.

11. Transfers of the employees, is one more reason why people can not work. The effect of change can be very significant on most human beings. To cope up with new place and yet produce results can be difficult.

12. The intent of the employers can also hamper the working of the employees. To cite an example again from the Insurance sector it is seen that the initial level employees are hired more for their natural data rather than their ability. The natural data is the personal contacts of a person in his domicile area. As soon as the data is consumed, he is treated as useless and thrown out.

13. Most people are unable to compartmentalize their lives. They bring their domestic problems to the office and while going

home they carry the organizational tensions to their homes. Such people fail on both fronts.

The list can go a mile further but it does not help. Ironically, the employer who pays the salaries is the worst affected party and it is his initiative which should create a proper and mutually acceptable atmosphere to extract work from his employees. The employers have to remind themselves that in spite of all the above factors, some of their employees are still producing dazzling results. How they do is what the employer should be interested in. They have to find out what can be done and apply it. Before the inevitable pink slip, a reminder to the employee of his first day in the office has helped quite a few organizations.

***

CHAPTER TWENTY-EIGHT

Why Me?

"Why me of all the people?" the question flashes in our minds whenever we feel that we are at the receiving end of the unfair treatment meted out by the world. The intensity of the question and the responses to the same question may vary with respect to our age and our acquired maturity or lack of it. The younger we are, we tend to react even overreact, but as we think when we grow older, we *respond* rather than react. The reason being that we begin to understand, that even though apparently, we may not be at fault, bad things can still happen to any of us.

From the moment one goes in the "Why me" mode, he opens doors to misery, compounding the already complex problem. The human mind is a fantastic library which has ready references for each of our negative and positive thoughts. It tends to give us supporting information for our thought process. Mind you that it does not decide the veracity of thought process. The best way to overcome such a state is to regroup, reassess and most importantly to start afresh. Those who do not do so, become confused and more likely de-motivated. As a result, they try to find a person they feel is better equipped to provide solutions. Again, whether the person is really worthwhile is a matter of chance. Very rarely what he tells differs from what our parents have already told us.

In a moment of weakness, one approaches some one who tells him that the present bad phase is due to the cosmic and star signs disturbances in his horoscope. The next stage is of self pity which to my mind is the lowest stage of human existence, and very few overcome this. Such persons simply forget the logic of numbers and the earlier instances where they were slightly lucky.

Human life has lot of complicated ranges and patterns in which a man tries to find his forte. Happy and sad, rich and poor, smart and clumsy, clever and dull, promise and fulfillment, success and failure are some of the common ranges which affect our daily lives. One of the most significant ranges is the range between the 'why me and why not me', when he tries to understand this complicated and often talked about range, he finds himself a little baffled.

The other side, where people are competing saying 'why not me', they volunteer, are ready to compete, not afraid of trying things others would not even think of, they are ready to fail while they try, they even fail and yet they are happy. They are ready to do the same exercise all over again till they succeed. During this time, they do not have time to be unhappy, morose. The solders on the front cannot think in terms of why me or why not me when they attack the enemy. They are focused and they achieve much more than an ordinary human being can even think of.

When a calamity strikes most people just go in to *why me* mode. They try to find reasons for being subjected to something uncommon, unthinkable. Very often they find people who are seemingly at their worse and yet not suffering. This becomes inexplicable and adds to the already miserable condition of the concerned person. Sometimes, a person who is a regular as far as exercise, diet, habits, life style and of a composed nature gets a stroke. While lying in ICCU he has two choices of why me or why not me. In the first case he goes in the *blame all stint* but in why not me mode he would start to adjust with changed matrix of his life. 'Why not me' people are may be better prepared for any eventuality, much better than their counterparts. Some one very rightly has said 'Good things come to those who wait, better things come to those who try and best things come to those who believe.' The faith or lack of it is the main reason for the state of mind even in the weirdest situations. One who has faith and ready to wait and at the same time keeps doing his regular chores is most likely to succeed.

What you have is *reality*, what you want is the *desire* and what you can do is your *destiny* so next time when you suffer a setback find out what best choices you have and do your best and get out with a spring in your step.

"Why bad things happen to good people?" a question that has never been properly answered. I say properly because many have tried to do so drawing richly from various religious texts. When we verify on a logical scale the answers seem inadequate. One of the very popular explanations is to tell a person that all his present suffering is a resultant of the bad deeds (*Dushkrits*) done by him in his earlier birth. If you want to check out the inadequacy, try telling this to a mother who has delivered a stillborn or to a father who is a victim of a dowry death of his daughter. All your wisdom filled words would be rendered useless. When words fail, a simple touch never fails.

The other great healer is the time. How, some one, some how manages to overcome and get back to routine, regain the balance is a matter of concern to all of us.

May be the best way is to tell the person: - "The sky is at its darkest just before the sunrise. All it takes a ray of light and hope to dispel the darkness. May be the God is still planning the best deal for you, so cheer up, my friend and smile"

***

CHAPTER TWENTY-NINE

'Why me' to 'why not me'

Human life has lot of complicated ranges and patterns in which a man tries to find his forte. Happy and sad, rich and poor, smart and clumsy, clever and dull, promise and fulfillment, success and failure are some of the common ranges which affect our daily lives. One of the most significant ranges is the range between the 'why me and why not me', when he tries to understand this complicated and often talked about range, he finds himself a little baffled.

The people in the why me range easily outnumber the why not me type and this is really a problem. 'Why me' people have a perennial unhappy atmosphere around them. "Why me of all the people?" the question flashes in our minds whenever we feel that we are at the receiving end of the unfair treatment meted out by the world. The intensity of the question and the responses to the same may vary with respect to our age. The younger we are, we tend to react even overreact, but as we think we grow older, we respond rather than react. The reason being that we begin to understand, that even though apparently, we may not be at fault, bad things can still happen to any of us.

From the moment one goes in the "Why me" mode, he opens doors to misery, compounding the already complex problem. The human mind is a fantastic library which has ready references for each of our negative and positive thoughts. It tends to give us supporting information for our thought process. Mind you that it does not decide the veracity of thought process. The best way to overcome such a state is to regroup, reassess and most importantly to start afresh. Those who do not do so, become confused and more likely de-motivated. As a result, they try to find a person they feel is better equipped to provide solutions. Again, whether the person is really worthwhile is a matter of chance. Very rarely what he tells differs from what our parents have already told us. The 'why me' usually deactivates, the last remains of the will to do some thing. In a moment of weakness, one approaches someone who tells him that the present bad phase is due to the cosmic and star signs disturbances in his horoscope. The next stage is of self pity which to my mind is the lowest stage of human existence, and very few overcome this. Such persons simply forget the logic of numbers and the earlier instances where they were slightly lucky.

The other side, where people are competing saying 'why not me', they volunteer, are ready to compete, not afraid of trying things others would not even think of, they are ready to fail while they try, they even fail and yet they are happy. They are ready to do the same exercise all over again till they succeed. During this time, they do not have time to be unhappy, morose. The solders on the front cannot think in terms of why me or why not me when they attack the enemy. They are focused and they achieve much more than an ordinary human being can even think of.

When a calamity strikes most people just go in to *why me* mode. They try to find reasons for being subjected to some thing uncommon, unthinkable. Very often they find people who are seemingly at their worse and yet not suffering. This becomes inexplicable and adds to the already miserable condition of the concerned person. Some times a person who is a regular as far as exercise, diet, habits, life style and composed nature concerned gets a stroke. While lying in ICCU he has two choices of why me or why not me. In the first case he goes in the blame all stint but in why not me mode he would start to adjust with changed matrix of his life. 'Why not me' people are may be better prepared for any eventuality, much better than their counterparts. Some one very rightly has said 'Good things come to those who wait, better things come to those who try and best things come to those who believe.'

The faith or lack of it is the main reason for the state of mind even in the weirdest situations. One who has faith and ready to wait and at the same time keeps doing his regular chores is most likely to succeed.

What you have is reality, what you want is the desire and what you can do is your destiny so next time when you suffer a setback find out what best choices you have and do your best and get out with a spring in your step.

    ***

www.ingramcontent.com/pod-product-compliance
Lightning Source LLC
Chambersburg PA
CBHW061319120726
48001CB00002B/589